Exile and Pride

Exile and Pride

Disability, Queerness and Liberation

Eli Clare

South End Press
Cambridge, MA

Any properly footnoted quotation of up to 500 sequential words may be used without permission, as long as the total number of words quoted does not exceed 2,000. For longer quotations or for a greater number of total words, please write for permission to South End Press.

Several chapters of this book have appeared elsewhere. "Clearcut: Explaining the Distance," "Clearcut: Brutes and Bumper Stickers," and "Clearcut: End of the Line" were all excerpted in *Orion* and appeared in full in *Agenda*. Earlier versions of "Losing Home" and "A Supercrip Story" were also published in *Agenda*. "Losing Home" originally appeared in *Queerly Classed: Gay Men and Lesbians Write about Class* (South End Press). An early version of "Stones in My Pockets, Stones in My Heart" was published in *Sojourner: The Women's Forum*. The poem fragment from "Angels" appeared in *Hanging Loose* and the fragment from "Tremors" was published in the anthology *My Lover Is a Woman: Contemporary Lesbian Love Poems*(Ballentine Books).

Cover design by Ellen P. Shapiro

Cover photographs © Photodisk, Inc.

Page design and production by the South End Press collective

Printed in the U.S.A. on acid-free paper

First edition

Library of Congress Cataloging-in-Publication Data
Clare, Eli.
    Exile and pride : disability, queerness, and liberation / Eli Clare.
        p.   cm.
    Includes bibliographical references and index.
    ISBN 0-89608-606-2 (alk. paper). — ISBN 0-89608-605-4 (pbk. : alk. paper)
    1. Clare, Eli. 2. Women political activists—United States Biography. 3. Cerebral palsied—United States Biography.
    I. Title.
    HQ1426.C56   1999
    305.48'916—dc21
    [B]   99-36063
                                                                    CIP

South End Press, 7 Brookline Street, Cambridge, MA 02139-4146

www.lbbs.org/sep/sep/htm

06 05 04 03 02 01 00 99   1 2 3 4 5 6 7 8

Contents

Acknowledgements

This book is grounded in community. Without the many people who read the endless drafts; who talked ideas, politics, activism, philosophy, and poetry with me; who encouraged my work in every possible way; who took to the streets with me; who stayed with me through the daily ups and downs; these words would simply not exist.

For seeing me and this book every step of way, I cannot thank Joanna Kadi enough. Through it all, Su Penn has been a wonderful writing buddy. My MFA advisors at Goddard College, Nora Mitchell and Jan Clausen, and my high school 'poetry teacher, Bill Beckman, led me toward this book. My dog, Jasper, reminded me over and over again that there is much more to life than my computer keyboard, insisting upon two walks a day and as many frolics in the woods as possible.

For support and sustenance of many kinds over the years, thanks to Jan Binder, Susan Cowling, David Dierauer, Kenny Fries, Aura Glaser, Jessica Hammond, Cheryl Hughes, Joanna Kadi, Karen Kerns, Sarra Levine, Andrea Freud Loewenstein, Annette Marcus, Kim McGinnis, Adrianne Neff, Claire Neff, Sarah Paige, Su Penn, Susan Raffo, Tovah Redwood, Merri Rose, Scott Solik, Gen Stewart, Chris Vaughn, and Laurie Wechter.

And finally thank you to the South End Press collective and my editor Loie Hayes, who knew when and where to push.

Please note that I have changed a few names and identifying details in the following pages to protect my privacy and the privacy of others.

—Eli Clare

Foreword

by Suzanne Pharr

The books that move us most are the ones that help us make sense of our experience, that take pieces of what we already know and put it together with new insights, new analysis, enabling us to form a fresh vision of ourselves and our lives. They resonate with our own experience and take us further into understanding by the courageous ways they name the truth. These are the books that increase our power. For me, Audre Lorde's *Sister Outsider* and Adrienne Rich's *On Lies, Secrets, & Silence* were such books, and there were significant others along the way that helped me think and see anew. And now there's Eli Clare's *Exile and Pride*.

Foremost, it is the work of a poet. It is the poet that searches for fresh language, the words that grip one's emotion while engaging the intellect, the words that struggle for essential truths in the heart and mind. It is the poet that gives this book a rhythm that returns us again and again to its central truth: there are no simple answers. Instead there are ambiguities and complexities in every person, in every politic, in every action.

Like the poet who sees all of life in a raindrop, Clare finds meaning for humankind in the life she lived as a disabled, mixed-class queer in Port Orford, Oregon, where the environment is ravaged by the needs of capitalism and local economic survival, where she was subjected to sexual violence by her father, where she learned to love nature and people and life, and where she found the necessity to embrace exile as her means of survival.

In *Exile and Pride*, Eli Clare has walked courageously into the troubled waters of class and economic injustice, a subject that is always shunted out of the national dialogue and is often on the periphery of the identity politics which dominate the progressive movement. She is masterful in her ability to recognize the full humanity of people who are forced to live in the contradictory position of loving the environment and of destroying it for their economic survival. She sees the economic struggle of the loggers and their anger, as well as the principles and often shortsightedness of the environmentalists who call the loggers "rednecks" and condemn them. More importantly, she goes right to the source of the conflict and names capitalistic greed and our supporting consumerism as causes of environmental destruction.

Exile and Pride brings me back to those intense feelings of ambivalence, ambiguity, and isolation that I felt in my 20s after I had left a Georgia dirt farm and graduated from a small, working-class women's college. I was torn between my rural self, and the farm community I loved, and the urban world that was giving me enough air to breathe so I could develop other sides of myself. I was in conflict over being a closeted queer girl who was in danger of rejection by family, church, and community; being a white girl in the middle of a civil rights movement that was not just about race but also about class; being a girl who loved farming but who had chosen to teach. In the graduate school at the University of Buffalo, everything I had come from was scorned: rural, redneck, Southern white. Once I had left my rural community, I felt I would never be able to live in peace with myself and my people again: I was in exile from large parts of myself and from my folks.

It has taken decades—and more than one liberation movement—or me to come home to myself and to them. Though the community no longer exists, neither its people nor its land—because Atlanta's sprawl has moved out to eat up farmland and trees and to replace them with shopping malls and housing developments—I can again find home with my family and the working-class people whose values and stories have shaped my life.

Exile and Pride also speaks to my own experiences related to disability and class. As I read her analysis of "supercrip," I thought of my friend Ann, who lived with the terrible, rare, degenerative disease Marie's ataxia. Every day for her was a struggle, not just for survival but for human dignity in a world that loved her when she was funny, courageous and defiant, but slammed, ignored, or shamed her when she was simply in pain or angry or stubborn or weak in body and spirit. Until her death, she struggled for the simple acceptance of herself as a full human being—weak and strong, complicated, sexual, loving, and angry.

What I appreciate most about *Exile and Pride* is the way that Eli Clare does not shy away from the ambiguity of issues, from her own ambivalence, from the complexity that does not permit easy or simple answers. She writes of a physical body that carries simultaneously disability and ability, strength and weakness—a fluctuation that defies stereotyping. "Ability" and "disability" define neither the limits nor possibilities of one's being. She tells of a father's sexual violence that is outrageous and destructive, and also of how he taught her to know the natural world and to use her strength to build houses. She writes of the brutality of her rural neighbors and their generosity, the destruction of the forests and the salmon runs by loggers and their love of the land, her love and dislike of urban life, her love of rural life, and her inability to find home there as a disabled queer.

It is this complex seeing, this complex analysis, that we so need. In a time of soundbites, sitcoms, and over-simplification of issues, we lose our ability to addresses multi-faceted problems with multi-faceted solutions. We find ourselves impatient and uncomfortable with problems that don't lend themselves to easy answers and actions; it becomes too hard for us to find empathy with aspects of the lives of the people we want to name as enemies. Taking the time to fully recognize complexity will lead us to different ways of dealing with problems: discussions, negotiations, compromises, a true democratic process. The other road, so often taken, is to demolish the good and bad together, to bomb a village in order to save it, to destroy a person in order to gain what we want. Eli Clare takes us on a journey up, down, and around the mountain, across the plains, and to the sea. She shows us ambiguities and complexities, but does not let them create an escape into confusion and inaction; instead, she points us toward a way of seeing and thinking that can lead us to a humane approach to political action.

–April 1999

Dedication

To the rocks and trees, hills and beaches

The Mountain

I: A Metaphor

The mountain as metaphor looms large in the lives of marginalized people, people whose bones get crushed in the grind of capitalism, patriarchy, white supremacy. How many of us have struggled up the mountain, measured ourselves against it, failed up there, lived in its shadow? We've hit our heads on glass ceilings, tried to climb the class ladder, lost fights against assimilation, scrambled toward that phantom called normality.

We hear from the summit that the world is grand from up there, that we live down here at the bottom because we are lazy, stupid, weak, and ugly. We decide to climb that mountain, or make a pact that our children will climb it. The climbing turns out to be unimaginably difficult. We are afraid; every time we look ahead we can find nothing remotely familiar or comfortable. We lose the trail. Our wheelchairs get stuck. We speak the wrong languages with the wrong accents, wear the wrong clothes, carry our bodies the wrong ways, ask the wrong questions, love the wrong people. And it's goddamn lonely up there on the mountain. We decide to stop climbing and build a new house right where we are. Or we decide to climb back down to the people we love, where the food, the clothes, the dirt, the sidewalk, the steaming asphalt under our feet, our crutches, all feel right. Or we find the path again, decide to continue climbing only to have the very people who told us how wonderful life is at the summit booby-trap the trail. They burn the bridge over the impassable canyon. They redraw our topo maps so that we end up walking in circles. They send their goons—those working-class and poor people they employ as their official brutes—to push us over the edge. Maybe we get to the summit, but probably not. And the price we pay is huge.

Up there on the mountain, we confront the external forces, the power brokers who benefit so much from the status quo and their privileged position at the very summit. But just as vividly, we come face-to-face with our own bodies, all that we cherish and despise, all that lies imbedded there. This I know because I have caught myself lurching up the mountain.

II: A Supercrip Story

I am a gimp, a crip, disabled with cerebral palsy. The story of me lurching up the mountain begins not on the mountain, but with one of the dominant images of disabled people, the supercrip. A boy without hands bats .486 on his Little League team. A blind man hikes the Appalachian Trail from end to end. An adolescent girl with Down's syndrome learns to drive and has a boyfriend. A guy with one leg runs across Canada. The nondisabled world is saturated with these stories: stories about gimps who engage in activities as grand as walking 2,500 miles or as mundane as learning to drive. They focus on disabled people "overcoming" our disabilities. They reinforce the superiority of the nondisabled body and mind. They turn individual disabled people, who are simply leading their lives, into symbols of inspiration.

Supercrip stories never focus on the conditions that make it so difficult for people with Down's to have romantic partners, for blind people to have adventures, for disabled kids to play sports. I don't mean medical conditions. I mean material, social, legal conditions. I mean lack of access, lack of employment, lack of education, lack of personal attendant services. I mean stereotypes and attitudes. I mean oppression. The dominant story about disability should be about ableism, not the inspirational supercrip crap, the believe-it-or-not disability story.

I've been a supercrip in the mind's eye of nondisabled people more than once. Running cross-country and track in high school, I came in dead last in more races than I care to count. My tense, wiry body, right foot wandering out to the side as I grew tired, pushed against the miles, the stopwatch, the final back stretch, the last muddy hill. Sometimes I was lapped by the front runners in races as short as the mile. Sometimes I trailed everyone on a cross-country course by two, three, four minutes. I ran because I loved to run, and yet after every race, strangers came to thank me, cry over me, tell me what an inspiration I was. To them, I was not just another hopelessly slow, tenacious high school athlete, but super-crip, tragic brave girl with CP, courageous cripple. It sucked. The slogan on one of my favorite t-shirts, black cotton inked with big fluorescent pink letters, one word per line, reads PISS ON PITY.

~~~

Me lurching up the mountain is another kind of supercrip story, a story about internalizing supercripdom, about becoming supercrip in my own mind's eye, a story about climbing Mount Adams last summer with my friend Adrianne. We had been planning this trip for years. Adrianne spent her childhood roaming New Hampshire's White Mountains and wanted to take me to her favorite haunts. Six times in six years, we set the trip up, and every time something fell through at the last minute. Finally, last summer everything stayed in place.

I love the mountains almost as much as I love the ocean, not a soft, romantic kind of love, but a deep down rumble in my bones. When Adrianne pulled out her trail guides and topo maps and asked me to choose one of the mountains we'd climb, I looked for a big mountain, for a long, hard hike, for a trail that would take us well above treeline. I picked Mount Adams. I think I asked Adrianne, "Can I handle this trail?" meaning, "Will I have to clamber across deep gulches on narrow log bridges without hand railings to get to the top of this mountain?" Without a moment's hesitation, she said, "No problem."

I have walked from Los Angeles to Washington, D.C., on a peace walk; backpacked solo in the southern Appalachians, along Lake Superior, on the beaches at Point Reyes; slogged my way over Cottonwood Pass and down South Manitou's dunes. Learning to walk took me longer than most kids—certainly most nondisabled kids. I was two and a half before I figured out how to stand on my own two feet, drop my heels to the ground, balance my weight on the whole long flat of each foot. I wore orthopedic shoes—clunky, unbending monsters—for several years, but never had to suffer through physical therapy or surgery. Today, I can and often do walk unending miles for the pure joy of walking. In the disability community I am called a walkie, someone who doesn't · use a wheelchair, who walks rather than rolls. Adrianne and I have been hiking buddies for years. I never questioned her judgment. Of course, I could handle Mount Adams.

The night before our hike, it rained. In the morning we thought we might have to postpone. The weather reports from the summit still looked uncertain, but by 10 a.m. the clouds started to lift, later than we had planned to begin but still okay. The first mile of trail snaked through steep jumbles of rock, leaving me breathing hard, sweat drenching my cotton t-shirt, dripping into my eyes. I love this pull and stretch, quads and calves, lungs and heart, straining.

~~~

The trail divides and divides again, steeper and rockier now, moving not around but over piles of craggy granite, mossy and a bit slick from the night's rain. I start having to watch where I put my feet. Balance has always been somewhat of a problem for me, my right foot less steady than my left. On uncertain ground, each step becomes a studied move, especially when my weight is balanced on my right foot. I take the trail slowly, bringing both feet together, solid on one stone, before leaning into my next step. This assures my balance, but I lose all the momentum gained from swinging into a step, touching ground, pushing off again in the same moment. There is no rhythm to my stop-and-go clamber. I know that going down will be worse, gravity underscoring my lack of balance. I watch Adrianne ahead of me hop from one rock to the next up this tumble trail of granite. I know that she's breathing hard, that this is no easy climb, but also that each step isn't a strategic game for her. I start getting scared as the trail steepens, then steepens again, the rocks not letting up. I can't think of how I will ever come down this mountain. Fear sets up a rumble right alongside the love in my bones. I keep climbing. Adrianne starts waiting for me every 50 yards or so. I finally tell her I'm scared.

She's never hiked this trail before so can't tell me if this is as steep as it gets. We study the topo map, do a time check. We have many hours of daylight ahead of us, but we're both thinking about how much time it might take me to climb down, using my hands and butt when I can't trust my feet. I want to continue up to treeline, the pines shorter and shorter, grown twisted and withered, giving way to scrub brush, then to lichen-covered granite, up to the sun-drenched cap where the mountains all tumble out toward the hazy blue horizon. I want to so badly, but fear rumbles next to love next to real lived physical limitations, and so we decide to turn around. I cry, maybe for the first time, over something I want to do, had many reasons to believe I could, but really can't. I cry hard, then get up and follow Adrianne back down the mountain. It's hard and slow, and I use my hands and butt often and wish I could use gravity as Adrianne does to bounce from one flat spot to another, down this jumbled pile of rocks.

~~~

I thought a lot coming down Mount Adams. Thought about bitterness. For as long as I can remember, I have avoided certain questions. Would I have been a good runner if I didn't have CP? Could I have been a surgeon or pianist, a dancer or gymnast? Tempting questions that have no answers. I refuse to enter the territory marked *bitterness*. I wondered about a friend who calls herself one of the last of the polio tribe, born just before the polio vaccine's discovery. Does she ever ask what her life might look like had she been born five years later? On a topo map, bitterness would be outlined in red.

I thought about the model of disability that separates impairment from disability. Disability theorist Michael Oliver defines impairment as "lacking part of or all of a limb, or having a defective limb, organism or mechanism of the body."[1] I lack a fair amount of fine motor control. My hands shake. I can't play a piano, place my hands gently on a keyboard, or type even 15 words a minute.

Whole paragraphs never cascade from my fingertips. My long-hand is a slow scrawl. I have trouble picking up small objects, putting them down. Dicing onions with a sharp knife puts my hands at risk. A food processor is not a yuppie kitchen luxury in my house, but an adaptive device. My gross motor skills are better but not great. I can walk mile after mile, run and jump and skip and hop, but don't expect me to walk a balance beam. A tightrope would be murder; boulder hopping and rock climbing, not much better. I am not asking for pity. I am telling you about impairment.

Oliver defines disability as "the disadvantage or restriction of activity caused by a contemporary social organisation which takes no or little account of people who have physical [and/or cognitive/developmental/mental] impairments and thus excludes them from the mainstream of society."[2] I write slowly enough that cashiers get impatient as I sign my name to checks, stop talking to me, turn to my companions, hand them my receipts. I have failed timed tests, important tests, because teachers wouldn't allow me extra time to finish the sheer physical act of writing, wouldn't allow me to use a typewriter. I have been turned away from jobs because my potential employer believed my slow, slurred speech meant I was stupid. Everywhere I go people stare at me, in restaurants as I eat, in grocery stores as I fish coins out of my pocket to pay the cashier, in parks as I play with my dog. I am not asking for pity. I am telling you about disability.

In large part, disability oppression is about access. Simply being on Mount Adams, halfway up Air Line Trail, represents a whole lot of access. When access is measured by curb cuts, ramps, and whether they are kept clear of snow and ice in the winter; by the width of doors and height of counters; by the presence or absence of Braille, closed captions, ASL, and TDDs; my not being able to climb all the way to the very top of Mount Adams stops being about disability. I decided that turning around before reaching the summit was more about impairment than disability.

But even as I formed the thought, I could feel my resistance to it. To neatly divide disability from impairment doesn't feel right. My experience of living with CP has been so shaped by ableism—or to use Oliver's language, my experience of impairment has been so shaped by disability—that I have trouble separating the two. I understand the difference between failing a test because some stupid school rule won't give me more time and failing to summit Mount Adams because it's too steep and slippery for my feet. The first failure centers on a socially constructed limitation, the second on a physical one.

At the same time, both center on my body. The faster I try to write, the more my pen slides out of control, muscles spasm, then contract trying to stop the tremors, my shoulder and upper arm growing painfully tight. Even though this socially constructed limitation has a simple solution—access to a typewriter, computer, tape recorder, or person to take dictation—I experience the problem on a very physical level. In the case of the bodily limitation, my experience is similarly physical. My feet simply don't know the necessary balance. I lurch along from one rock to the next, catching myself repeatedly as I start to fall, quads quickly sore from exertion, tension, lack of momentum. These physical experiences, one caused by a social construction, the other by a bodily limitation, translate directly into frustration, making me want to crumple the test I can't finish, hurl the rocks I can't climb. This frustration knows no neat theoretical divide between disability and impairment. Neither does disappointment nor embarrassment. On good days, I can separate the anger I turn inward at my body from the anger that needs to be turned outward, directed at the daily ableist shit, but there is nothing simple or neat about kindling the latter while transforming the former. I decided that Oliver's model of disability makes theoretical and political sense but misses important emotional realities.

I thought of my nondisabled friends who don't care for camping, hiking, or backpacking. They would never spend a vacation sweat-drenched and breathing hard halfway up a mountain. I started to list their names, told Adrianne what I was doing. She reminded me of other friends who enjoy easy day hikes on smooth, well-maintained trails. Many of them would never even attempt the tumbled trail of rock I climbed for an hour and a half before turning around. We added their names to my list. It turned into a long roster. I decided that if part of what happened to me up there was about impairment, another part was about desire, my desire to climb mountains.

I thought about supercrips. Some of us—the boy who bats .486, the man who through-hikes the A.T.—accomplish something truly extraordinary and become supercrips. Others of us—the teen-ager with Down's who has a boyfriend, the kid with CP who runs track and cross-country—lead entirely ordinary lives and still become supercrips. Nothing about having a boyfriend or running cross-country is particularly noteworthy. Bat .486 or have a boy-friend, it doesn't matter; either way we are astonishing. In the creation of supercrip stories, nondisabled people don't celebrate any particular achievement, however extraordinary or mundane. Rather, these stories rely upon the perception that disability and achievement contradict each other and that any disabled person who overcomes this contradiction is heroic.

To believe that achievement contradicts disability is to pair helplessness with disability, a pairing for which crips pay an awful price. The nondisabled world locks us away in nursing homes. It deprives us the resources to live independently.[3] It physically and sexually abuses us in astoundingly high numbers.[4] It refuses to give us jobs because even when a workplace is accessible, the speech impediment, the limp, the ventilator, the seeing-eye dog are read as signs of inability.[5] The price is incredibly high.

~~~

And here, supercrip turns complicated. On the other side of super-cripdom lies pity, tragedy, and the nursing home. Disabled people know this, and in our process of knowing, some of us internalize the crap. We make supercrip our own, particularly the type that pushes into the extraordinary, cracks into our physical limitations. We use supercripdom as a shield, a protection, as if this individual internalization could defend us against disability oppression.

I climbed Mount Adams for an hour and a half scared, not sure I'd ever be able to climb down, knowing that on the next rock my balance could give out, and yet I climbed. Climbed surely be-cause I wanted the summit, because of the love rumbling in my bones. But climbed also because I wanted to say, "Yes, I have CP, but see. See, watch me. I can climb mountains too." I wanted to prove myself once again. I wanted to overcome my CP.

Overcoming has a powerful grip. Back home, my friends told me, "But you can walk any of us under the table." My sister, a serious mountain climber who spends many a weekend high up in the North Cascades, told me, "I bet with the right gear and enough practice you *could* climb Mount Adams." A woman who doesn't know me told Adrianne, "Tell your friend not to give up. She can do anything she wants. She just has to want it hard enough." I told myself as Adrianne and I started talking about another trip to the Whites, "If I used a walking stick, and we picked a dry day and a different trail, maybe I could make it up to the top of Adams." I never once heard, "You made the right choice when you turned around." The mountain just won't let go.

III: Home

I will never find home on the mountain. This I know. Rather home starts here in my body, in all that lies imbedded beneath my skin. My disabled body: born prematurely in the backwoods of Oregon, I was first diagnosed as "mentally retarded," and then later as having CP. I grew up to the words *cripple, retard, monkey, defect*, took all the staring into me and learned to shut it out.

My body violated: early on my father started raping me, physically abusing me in ways that can only be described as torture, and sharing my body with other people, mostly men, who did the same. I abandoned that body, decided to be a hermit, to be done with humans, to live among the trees, with the salmon, to ride the south wind bareback.

My white body: the only person of color in my hometown was an African-American boy, adopted by a white family. I grew up to persistent rumors of a lynching tree way back in the hills, of the sheriff running people out of the county. For a long time after moving to the city, college scholarship in hand, all I could do was gawk at the multitude of humans: homeless people, their shopping carts and bedrolls, Black people, Chinese people, Chicanos, drag queens and punks, vets down on Portland's Burnside Avenue, white men in their wool suits, limos shined to sparkle. I watched them all, sucking in the thick weave of Spanish, Cantonese, street talk, English. This is how I became aware of my whiteness.

My queer body: I spent my childhood, a tomboy not sure of my girlness, queer without a name for my queerness. I cut firewood on clearcuts, swam in the river, ran the beaches at Battle Rock and Cape Blanco. When I found dykes, fell in love for the first time, came into a political queer community, I felt as if I had found home again.

The body as home, but only if it is understood that bodies are never singular, but rather haunted, strengthened, underscored by countless other bodies. My alcoholic, Libertarian father and his father, the gravedigger, from whom my father learned his violence. I still dream about them sometimes, ugly dreams that leave me panting with fear in the middle of the night. One day I will be done with them. The white, working-class loggers, fishermen, and ranchers I grew up among: Les Smith, John Black, Walt Maya. Their ways of dressing, moving, talking helped shape my sense of self. Today when I hear queer activists say the word *redneck* like a cuss word, I think of those men, backs of their necks turning red in the summertime from long days of work outside, felling trees, pulling fishnets, baling hay. I think of my butchness, grounded there, overlaid by a queer, urban sensibility. A body of white, rural, working-class values. I still feel an allegiance to this body, even as I reject the virulent racism, the unexamined destruction of forest and river. How could I possibly call my body home without the bodies of trees that repeatedly provided me refuge? Without queer bodies? Without crip bodies? Without transgendered and transsexual bodies? Without the history of disabled people who worked as freaks in the freak show, displaying their bodies: Charles Stratton posed as General Tom Thumb, Hiriam and Barney Davis billed as the "Wild Men from Borneo"? The answer is simple. I couldn't.

The body as home, but only if it is understood that place and community and culture burrow deep into our bones. My earliest and most enduring sense of place is in the backwoods of Oregon, where I grew up but no longer live, in a logging and fishing town of a thousand that hangs on to the most western edge of the continental United States. To the west stretches the Pacific Ocean; to the east the Siskiyou Mountains rise, not tall enough to be mountains but too steep to be hills. Portland is a seven-hour drive north; San Francisco, a twelve-hour drive south. Home for me is marked by Douglas fir and chinook salmon, south wind whipping the ocean into a fury of waves and surf. Marked by the aching knowledge of environmental destruction, the sad truth of that town founded on the genocide of Native peoples, the Tuni and Coquille, Talkemas and Latgawas. In writing about the backwoods and the rural, white, working-class culture found there, I am not being nostalgic, reaching backward toward a re-creation of the past. Rather I am reaching toward my bones. When I write about losing that place, about living in exile, I am putting words to a loss which also grasps at my bones.

The body as home, but only if it is understood that language too lives under the skin. I think of the words *crip, queer, freak, redneck*. None of these are easy words. They mark the jagged edge between self-hatred and pride, the chasm between how the dominant culture views marginalized peoples and how we view ourselves, the razor between finding home, finding our bodies, and living in exile, living on the metaphoric mountain. Whatever our relationships with these words—whether we embrace them or hate them, feel them draw blood as they hit our skin or find them entirely fitting, refuse to say them or simply feel uncomfortable in their presence— we deal with their power every day. I hear these words all the time. They are whispered in the mirror as I dress to go out, as I straighten my tie and shrug into my suit jacket; on the streets as folks gawk at my trembling hands, stare trying to figure out whether I'm a woman or man; in half the rhetoric I hear from environmentalists and queer activists, rhetoric where rural working-class people get cast as clods and bigots. At the same time, I use some, but not all, of these words to call out my pride, to strengthen my resistance, to place myself within community. *Crip, queer, freak, redneck* burrowed into my body.

The body as home, but only if it is understood that bodies can be stolen, fed lies and poison, torn away from us. They rise up around me—bodies stolen by hunger, war, breast cancer, AIDS, rape; the daily grind of factory, sweatshop, cannery, sawmill; the lynching rope; the freezing streets; the nursing home and prison. African-American drag performer Leonard/Lynn Vines, walking through his Baltimore neighborhood, called a "drag queen faggot bitch" and shot six times. Matt Sheppard—gay, white, young— tied to a fence post in Wyoming and beaten to death. Some bodies are taken for good; other bodies live on, numb, abandoned, full of self-hate. Both have been stolen. Disabled people cast as supercrips and tragedies; lesbian/gay/bisexual/trans people told over and over again that we are twisted and unnatural; poor people made responsible for their own poverty. Stereotypes and lies lodge in our bodies as surely as bullets. They live and fester there, stealing the body.

The body as home, but only if it is understood that the stolen body can be reclaimed. The bodies irrevocably taken from us: we can memorialize them in quilts, granite walls, candlelight vigils; remember and mourn them; use their deaths to strengthen our will. And as for the lies and false images, we need to name them, transform them, create something entirely new in their place, something that comes close and finally true to the bone, entering our bodies as liberation, joy, fury, hope, a will to refigure the world. The body as home.

~~~

The mountain will never be home, and still I have to remember it grips me. Supercrip lives inside my body, ready and willing to push the physical limitations, to try the "extraordinary," because down at the base of the mountain waits a nursing home. I hang on to a vision. Someday after the revolution, disabled people will live ordinary lives, neither heroic nor tragic. *Crip, queer, freak, redneck* will be mere words describing human difference. Supercrip will be dead; the nursing home, burnt down; the metaphoric mountain, collapsed in volcanic splendor. Post-revolution I expect there will still be literal mountains I want to climb and can't, but I'll be able to say without doubt, without hesitation, "Let's turn around here. This one is too steep, too slippery for my feet."

I: PLACE

Water warmed all day and still cold, I lay
my body in the riffle where stream
meets river, let the current pull, finger bones
tremble. Hang onto the rocky bottom
long as I can, then give way, body
rushing downstream to steadier water.

—from "Angels"

Clearcut:
Explaining the
Distance

1979. Each day after school I run the six miles from Highway 101 to my house. The road follows Elk River. I pass the dairy farm, the plywood mill that burned down three years ago, the valley's volunteer fire department station, the boat landing where recreational fishermen put in their boats during salmon season. I have the curves and hills memorized, tick the miles off, skin salty with sweat, lungs working a hard rhythm. I know most of the people who drive by. They wave and swerve into the other lane. The logging trucks honk as they rumble by loaded with 10 or 15 skinny logs. I remember when one or two huge logs made a load. Pushing up the last big hill, my lungs and legs begin to ache. Two curves before my house, I pass a yellow and brown sign. It reads: *United States Forest Service. Entering the Siskiyou National Forest.*

~~~

1994. I live now in southeast Michigan on the edge of corn country. Book-browsing I happen upon *Clearcut: The Tragedy of Industrial Forestry.*[1] The book documents clearcut logging throughout the United States and Canada. I glance at the big, full-color photos of new clearcuts, second growth forests, old growth forests, and tree farms; read the captions and descriptions. The book is divided by state and province. I look for Oregon and suddenly find myself in the Siskiyous, the photograph overwhelmingly familiar. The ground is bare, heaps of branches, stumps, and half logs hanging to the slope. There are no standing trees, only snatches of green, the new sprouts of huckleberry, greasewood, gorse, and tansy ragwort.

I used to cut firewood on clearcuts like this one. Upriver near Butler Basin and Bald Mountain after the last logs were driven away, loggers bulldozed the remains—branches, shattered logs, trees too small to buck into logs, stumps—into one enormous pile. Rather than burn these remains, the U.S. Forest Service issued firewood cutting permits. My father and I would spend the whole month of October on these clearcuts, gathering our winter's supply of firewood. He'd cut the logs into rounds, silver bar of chainsaw slicing through the wood, spewing sawdust. I'd watch his hands holding the saw steady, knowing its vibrations were climbing his arms, my ears full of the idle and roar.

I turn from the photo to the accompanying text. Photographer Elizabeth Feryl writes:

> While in the Port Orford, Oregon area, I'd heard of a slide along Bear Creek, so I decided to investigate. Nothing could have prepared me for the estimated 40,000 tons of mud, rock, and logging debris that had been dumped on the road and littered in the waterway. This "blow out," caused by the headwall of the drainage giving way, had also carved a swath through the hillside thirty feet deep, sixty feet across, and a half mile long taking the drainage down to the bedrock. We followed this carnage about a quarter of a mile to the "belly of the beast," the clearcut pictured here.[2]

Forty thousand tons of rock, mud, and logging debris to be washed downstream from Disaster Creek to Bear Creek to Bald Mountain Creek to Elk River to the Pacific Ocean. Elk River: river of my poems, real and metaphor; river of my childhood where I swam, skipped rocks, watched heron and salmon, learned to paddle a canoe. I read and reread the place names and the explanation. On steep slopes, trees literally hold the earth in place, and thus, clearcutting can destabilize whole mountainsides, inviting catastrophic slides called blowouts. I know all this but can't stop reading.

~~~

Later, I tell a friend about finding this photo. She has never walked a logging road, listened to the idle and roar of a chainsaw, or counted growth rings on an old growth stump, but we share a sensibility about environmental destruction. I describe the photo, explain blowouts, talk about watershed. What I don't say is how homesick I feel for those place names, plant names, bare slopes, not nostalgic, but lonely for a particular kind of familiarity, a loneliness that reaches deep under my skin, infuses my muscles and tendons. How do I explain the distance, the tension, the disjunction between my politics and my loneliness? She asks, "If you went for a walk along Elk River now, what changes would you notice?" I try to describe the images that have rumbled around my head for days. That winter, the river must have flooded chalky brown over the gravel bars. The next summer, the kids who lived near the river must have found their swimming holes changed, the deep pools shallower, current running faster. I describe spawning season at the confluence of Elk River and Anvil Creek. Salmon flounder into the creek, thrash up the shallows, dig nests in the gravel, flood the water with spawn. They are almost dead, bodies covered with white rot, the gravel bars littered with their carcasses. The following summer the river teems with coho and chinook fingerlings, three inches long, as they head downstream to the ocean. I can barely register that the spawning bed at Anvil Creek might be silted in with rock, mud, and logging debris, might not exist anymore.

~~~

For years I have wanted to write this story, have tried poems, diatribes, and theories. I've failed mostly because I haven't been able to bridge the chasm between my homesickness for a place thousands of miles away in the middle of logging country and my urban-created politics that have me raging at environmental destruction. I have felt lonely and frustrated. Without the words for this story, I lose part of myself into the chasm.

I am the child who grew up in the Siskiyou National Forest, in second growth woods that won't be logged again for a long time. The hills weren't replanted in the '40s and '50s when they were first clearcut and so grew back in a mix of alder, tan oak, myrtle, and madrone, trees the timber industry considers worthless. I played endlessly in this second growth forest. Followed the stream from our house uphill to the little dam where we siphoned water off to the holding tanks that supplied our house with water year-round. I loved taking the covers off the tanks, listening to the

trickle of water, watching the reflection of trees waver in the cool
dark surface. I drank big gulps straight from the tanks, my cheeks
and chin growing cold and wet. Then continued uph'll, kicking
through the alder and tan oak leaves, scrambling up slippery shale
slides. I pulled the bark off madrone trees in curly red strips, crum-
pled myrtle leaves to smell their pungent bay leaf odor. I knew
where the few remaining old growth firs still stood. Had my favorite climbing trees—white fir, grand fir, myrtle. I'd wrap my hands
around their branches, skin against bark, and pull my body up,
clambering toward sky, resting in the cradles where branch met
trunk. Or I'd stay on the ground, lean back into the unmovable
tower of trees. I walked out onto rotten logs that spanned the
stream, crouched down to examine moss, liverwort, lichen, shelf
mushrooms, tried to name the dozen shades of green, tan, and
brown, poked at snails and banana slugs. In the summer the hills
were hot and dry, the sun reaching easily through the trees. I
scrambled across clearings tangled in berry brambles and gorse,
through and around undergrowth, uphill to the rock out of which
the stream dripped.

I grew up to the high whine of diesel donkeys and chainsaws,
yarders and cats[3] next ridge over, the endless clatter of plywood
mill two miles downstream. When the warning whistle squealed
through the valley, I knew that logs were being pulled up out of
the gullies toward the loading areas where empty logging trucks
waited. I grew up to the sweet smell of damp wood chips being
hauled north on Highway 101 to the port in Coos Bay or the paper mill in Gardiner. I watched for hours as gigantic blowing machines loaded mountains of wood chips onto freighters bound for
Japan. I reveled in plant names: huckleberry, salmonberry, blackberry, salal, greasewood, manzanita, scotch broom, foxglove, lu-
pine, rhododendron, vine maple, alder, tan oak, red cedar, white
cedar, Port Orford cedar. I wanted a name for everything. I still
have a topographical map of the Elk River watershed, each quad-
rant carefully taped to the next.

I am the backpacker whose favorite trails now wind through
old growth rain forest, trees standing so tall I can't find their tops
wide, bark deeply grooved, ropy, fire-scarred. The sun barely
reaches through the canopy, leaving small pools of light on a forest

floor layered inches deep in fir and spruce needles. Everything cascades green, moss upon moss, swordtail ferns sprouting from rotten logs. The trail bends again and again around Sitka spruce, their roots sticking up high above ground, knobby and twisted. There is no undergrowth, only a thousand shades of green. Among these trees, I find a quiet.

I am the activist who has never poured sugar into a cat's gas tank but knows how. The activist who has never spent a night in the top of a Douglas fir slated for felling the next morning but would. The activist who has never blockaded a logging site or a logging executive's office as I have military complexes. I am the socialist with anarchist leanings who believes the big private timber corporations, like Weyerhaeuser and Georgia-Pacific, are corrupt, and the government agencies, like the U.S. Forest Service, that control public land are complicit. I am the adult who still loves the smell of wood chips, the roar of a lumber mill, who knows out-of-work loggers and dying logging towns. Living now on the edge of corn country, I am the writer who wants to make sense.

~~~

In the white, Western world view that I learned as a child, trees, fish, and water were renewable resources. Only 50 years prior, they were conceived of as endless resources, a myth white people brought west into the "frontier." Sometimes when I hiked upriver toward Butler Bar and saw ridge after ridge covered with alder and tan oak, mixed with Douglas fir and Sitka spruce, I believed trees were endless. Or when I went to the cannery and saw a day's catch of coho and chinook, I thought fish were endless. Particularly in the middle of winter when rain drenched the valley every day, I knew water was endless.

But in the 1960s and '70s, the powers-that-be in the public schools, government, and industry taught us that trees and fish, rather than being endless, were renewable. If clearcuts were diligently replanted, we would never run out of trees, paper, or lumber. If the salmon runs were carefully maintained by hatcheries, we would never run out of salmon. No one even bothered to explain about water.

Clearcuts, our teachers said, were good. They encouraged the growth of fir and pine, the so-called good—meaning profitable—trees that as seedlings need direct sunlight to grow. The practice of replanting and the superiority of tree farms were placed at the center of these lessons. But our teachers went far beyond trees in their defense of clearcut logging. Clearcuts, my classmates and I were told, provided bountiful browsing for deer and other wildlife. Hunters and their supporters quickly added that because this abundance of food, coupled with the disappearance of predators, led to a cycle of overpopulation, deer hunting was not just a sport, but a necessity. And so our world view developed, layer by layer. How did the forest and its wildlife ever survive before clearcutting, replanting, and sport hunting? We didn't ask because we were children taught not to question. We believed the propaganda.

No one told us about old growth forest. They didn't say, "Understand, a tree farm differs from an old growth forest." We didn't study the cycle of an ecosystem that depends upon rotting logs on the forest floor and a tree canopy hundreds of feet high—a cycle neither static nor altogether predictable, interrupted sometimes by fire, climate changes, or major volcanic activity, but nonetheless a cycle. I knew big, old trees existed. I remember the winter my favorite fir blew down. After we cut it into firewood, I hunkered down by the stump and counted its growth rings, one for every year of its life. It was 400 years old. But I didn't know about thousands of acres of big old trees. Nor did I know about animals, like the northern spotted owl, that live in old growth forests. No one told us, and the logging industry had quite a stake in the silence.

~~~

1979. I am part of the Youth Conservation Corps, a summer work program for teenagers. All summer we have made trails, picked up trash, maintained campgrounds, and built fences in the Siusilaw National Forest. This week we are camped east of Mapleton, near a ten-year-old tree farm, thinning the trees. Each morning we fan out into the woods to cut down all the trees four inches or less in diameter. The remaining trees will grow faster and bigger. In 30 or 40 years the U.S. Forest Service will bid these acres out to some private company to clearcut and then replant. I am learning to swing an ax, to know what angle to start a cut at, when to stop chopping and let gravity do the rest, how to pull a tree all the way down to the ground so it won't lean against neighboring trees and kill them. It's hot, dirty work. A girl on my crew went back to camp early yesterday after she stumbled into a bees' nest and was stung 30 times. Everyone thinks I'm nuts for liking this job. At lunch I sharpen my ax, the file flat against the beveled cutting edge. I like the weight of its wooden handle balanced on my shoulder as I trudge up and down the hills. I like touching the trees as I walk by, hands growing dark with pitch. I like the way my arms feel, aching but loose, at the end of the day. The sun is hot against my hard hat. Sweat collects under its band. I can smell the woods on my skin.

~~~

Along with trees, I studied salmon, fascinated with their three-year life cycle from spawning bed to ocean back to spawning bed. Most of what I knew came from the salmon hatchery two miles upriver of my house. In the winter I stood at the fish ladder waiting for fish to come leaping up the cascading stairs of water, then went to count the big scarred animals in their holding tanks. Sometimes I visited the lab where the biologists held the spawn and incubated the fertilized eggs. In the summer I rode my bike around the holding ponds and watched Glen and Paul feed the fingerlings, their hands dipping into five gallon buckets of feed, sweeping through the air, water coming alive as the fish jumped to catch the pellets. Other times I went across the river to the spawning bed at Anvil Creek. I knew two kinds of salmon existed, hatchery salmon and wild salmon. I thought they were the same, just as I thought a tree farm and an old growth forest were the same.

I didn't know why hatchery salmon needed to be grown in Elk River. I knew dams on the Columbia and urban pollution in the Willamette had nearly destroyed the salmon runs in those rivers, but there were no dams and minimal pollution on Elk River. The propaganda that passed as outdoor education didn't speak of the effects of clearcutting on salmon habitat. No one explained that as spawning beds silt up with logging debris and disappear, fewer and fewer wild salmon can spawn. I never heard that if the trees shading a creek are cut, the direct sunlight warms the water. And if the water temperature rises enough in a watershed, salmon, which require relatively cold water to survive, are put at risk. Nor did the propaganda speak of over-fishing. The commercial salmon fishermen who made their livelihoods fishing the summer salmon runs off the coast of California, Oregon, Washington, British Columbia, and Alaska hadn't yet heard of sustainable yield. The salmon runs seemed endless.

The powers-that-be didn't teach us that hatchery salmon differ from wild salmon, that they are genetically more homogeneous, more susceptible to disease, and less hardy once at sea. To raise salmon year after year in a hatchery, biologists use formaldehyde and other chemicals each summer to combat recurring diseases that kill thousands of hatchery fingerlings. The continuous pumping of water from the river into the hatchery's complex of tanks and back to the river washes these chemicals into the ecosystem. And each winter when hatchery salmon don't return to the hatchery in large enough numbers, biologists go to natural spawning beds and net wild salmon, taking them to the hatchery to augment their supply of spawn. Soon wild salmon might not exist. The propaganda neglected these details.

My classmates and I were taught by teachers who worked for schools funded largely with timber taxes; by U.S. Forest Service rangers and their brochures; and by industry-supported textbooks, displays, slide shows, and tours. The point isn't simply that we, like schoolchildren across the country, were taught half-truths about trees and salmon. Rather we learned even more fundamental lessons, that trees and salmon are endlessly renewable commodities. This view of the natural world, which puts clearcutting, replanting, and hatcheries at its center, conveniently supported the two industries, logging and fishing, that sustained the towns we lived in.

Not until I left Port Orford did I come into contact with other world views. Living in a city for the first time, I met people who knew salmon only as frozen patties, who used paper but had never been to a paper mill. For them trees were the tall, skinny maples, oaks, and beeches that grew along sidewalks. They navigated the seemingly impossible parking structures and bus stops with ease and comfort. Some of them believed that trees and salmon were more than commodities.

They created a fuzzy, romanticized version of nature, combining memories of Walt Disney nature movies with their occasional summer vacations to overcrowded national parks. Or they believed in a white urban version of tree spirits and Mother Earth. Either way, my new acquaintances held trees and fish in an awe-struck reverence as they talked about the dangers of nuclear power and the destruction of rain forests in Brazil, about clearcutting as rape. I simply listened. Surrounded by concrete and highrises, I slowly stopped taking the familiar plants and animals of the Siskiyou National Forest for granted. When I returned home to visit, I caught glimpses of what was beautiful and extraordinary about the place I grew up in, and what was ugly and heart-breaking. I started to believe that trees and salmon weren't just harvestable crops. I read Sierra Club literature, the *Earth First! Journal*, Dave Foreman's ecotage manual;[4] learned about Love Canal, Three Mile Island, the Nevada Test Site, Big Mountain; and started to turn from a right-wing, Libertarian-influenced childhood toward a progressive adulthood. I never grew into the white urban reverence of tree spirits and Mother Earth, a reverence often stolen from Native spiritual traditions and changed from a demanding, reciprocal relationship with the world into something naive and shallow that still places human life and form at its center. Nor did I ever grow comfortable with the metaphor of clearcutting as rape, the specificity of both acts too vivid for me to ever compare or conflate them. But I did come to believe that trees and fish are their own beings, important in and of themselves, and that I—as activist, consumer, and human being among the many beings on this planet—have a deeply complex relationship with them.

The people in Port Orford who had known me since I was born—Les Smith, the retired logger who ran the Port and Starboard Pizza Parlor; Venita Marstall, the cashier at True Value Hardware; Gerla Marsh, the teller at First Interstate Bank—no longer really knew me. I treasured the anonymity of the city and relished the multitude of cultures, ideas, and differences I encountered there. But still I ached for the trees, the river, the steep, quiet Siskiyous.

~~~

1989. I am backpacking alone on Washington's Olympic Penin-sula. I have spent the last week camping on the beach near Hole-in-the-Wall, reading and writing, letting high and low tide shape my days. Now I am camped at a state park, amidst new clearcuts. I replenished my food supply at Forks, a familiar little logging town, five or six one-ton pickups parked outside the chainsaw shop. I caught a ride to this campground with a man who works as a hoedad, replanting clearcuts. I am planning a three-day hike in the old growth rain forest before I head back to Seattle. I can never get enough of the big, old trees.

In the morning I set out for the trailhead. The logging road I'm on follows the Bogacheil River, winding through rolling pas-tures and second growth forest, that familiar mix of alder, tan oak, and fir. I hear chainsaws idle and roar the next ridge over. For a time I hear the logging trucks on Highway 101 downshift as they chug up a hill. I hear the high whine of the warning whistle. I ha-ven't heard these sounds in years. They mean home even as I re-mind myself about Weyerhaeuser, their union-busting tactics, their language of timber management, their defense of environmental destruction. A great blue heron startles me as it lifts off, flapping downstream on dusky blue wings. Home is also the damp, rotting log smell, the fog lifting to broken sun and wind. I am climbing steadily now, the two-lane shale road narrowing.

I round the next bend and am suddenly in a new clearcut: stumps as far as I can see, the great heap of tree parts left behind, bulldozer tracks frozen into the dry mud. I don't want this to mean destruction but rather to be home. I strain toward the memories of happy, exhausting trips to Butler Basin to cut fire-wood, sweat-drenched days east of Mapleton learning to swing an ax. Instead I see a graveyard, a war zone, the earth looking naked and torn. I imagine tree ghosts as real as crows. Whatever meta-phor I use, this is what white people have done to North America for 500 years—laid the land bare in the name of profit and pro-gress. I walk a mile, then two, knowing that I am seeing for the first time, seeing not as an outsider, a tourist horrified by some surface ugliness, but as someone who grew up in this graveyard, seeing with both my adult politics and my childhood loyalties, seeing through a lens of tension and contradiction. I climb up onto a stump and count its growth rings, trace the drought seasons marked by tight rings wrapped close together, the wet seasons marked by loose rings spaced farther apart. I want to rage and mourn, but instead I feel ordinary, matter-of-fact, as if the war zone can't touch my heart. I walk, waiting for my bone marrow to catch up to my politics. I walk numb, no longer in my body, unable to contain the tug-of-war between what is home and what is war zone. I round another bend, and am suddenly back in second growth forest.

I find the trailhead. These trees are marked every 50 feet with neon pink ribbon. Markers for a new road? A profit assessment? I tear the ribbon off each tree, stuff the plastic into a pocket, raging now at the impending destruction, at the audacity of neon pink amidst all the green. I cross a stream on a narrow moss-grown bridge. And then I am in old growth forest, national park land. It has started to rain softly. I sit, sheltered under a western red cedar, and eat my lunch, press my back into the thick, gray bark. The lines between old growth, second growth, and clearcut are sudden and unmistakable.

~~~

I live in a very different landscape now. The land is flat and open. The trees lose their leaves in an explosion of red, yellow, and orange every fall; regrow them in a burst of green every spring. In winter the snow comes wet and heavy, lining all the trees, or light and dry, drifting in billows. The green here isn't layered and shaded in a thousand varieties. Often I hunger for the ocean, the spawning beds, Douglas fir, rain that blows horizontally across the hills. I have filled my house with photographs, maps, stones, shells, sand dollars, fir cones, and wood to remind me of the landscape I still call home, a landscape that includes the sights, sounds, and smells of logging and commercial fishing.

Losing Home

I must find the words to speak of losing home. Then I never want to utter them again. They throb like an abscessed tooth, simply hurt too much. *Homesick* is a platitude. I need to grab at seemingly unrelated words. *Queer. Exile. Class.* I reach for my red and gold *American Heritage Dictionary* but restrain myself. I know the definitions. I need to enter the maze created by dyke identity, class location, and rural roots.

Let me start with *queer*, the easiest point of entry. In its largest sense, queer has always been where I belong. A girl child not convinced of her girlness. A backwoods hick in the city. A dyke in a straight world. A gimp in an ableist world. The eldest child of a poor father and a working-class mother, both teachers who tried to pull themselves up by their own bootstraps, using luck and white-skin privilege.

In its narrower sense, queer has been home since I became conscious of being a dyke. At age 17, I left the backwoods of Oregon with a high school diploma and a scholarship to college, grateful not to have a baby or a husband. A year later, after months of soul-searching, I finally realized that I was a dyke and had been for years. Since then, I have lived among dykes and created chosen families and homes, not rooted in geography, but in shared passion, imagination, and values. Our collective dyke household in Oakland with its vegetable garden in the front yard and chicken coop in the back. The women's circle on the Great Peace March from Los Angeles to Washington, D.C. The Women's Encampment for a Future of Peace and Justice in upstate New York. Queer potlucks in Ann Arbor, where I now live. Whether I've been walking across the country for peace or just hanging out listening to lesbian gossip, learning to cook tofu, or using red-handled bolt cutters to cut fence at the Army Depot, being a dyke in dyke community is as close as I've ever felt to belonging. And still I feel queer.

Exile. If *queer* is the easiest, then *exile* is the hardest. I lie when I write that home is being a dyke in dyke community. Rather, home is particular wild and ragged beaches, specific kinds of trees and berry brambles, the exact meander of the river I grew up near, the familiar sounds and sights of a dying logging and fishing town. Exile is the hardest because I have irrevocably lost that place as actual home. Let me return to *queer.*

Queer people—using the narrow definition—don't live in Port Orford, or at least I have never found them. And if we did, we would have to tolerate a lack of community, unspoken disdain, a wicked rumor mill, and the very real possibility of homophobic violence. Now if I moved back and lived quietly, never saying the word *dyke* but living a woman-centered life, no one would shoot at my house, throw stones through my windshield, or run me out of town. Muscles Smith at the cannery, Bonnie Wagner at the one-room library, and Dick Tucker at the lumber mill would just shake their heads and talk about Bob Craig's oldest back from the city. As long as I maintained the balance—my unspoken queerness weighed against their tacit acceptance—I would be fine.

Urban, middle-class queer activists may mock this balance as simply another "don't ask, don't tell" situation contributing to queer invisibility. While I agree that it isn't the ideal relationship between queer people and straight people, it is far better than the polite and disdainful invisibility bestowed on us by many middle-class, liberal heterosexuals. If you don't believe me, let me take you to my maternal grandfather's funeral. At the service I sat with family, my sister to the right, my great aunt Esther to the left, my aunt Margaret in front of us, her lover of many years to her right. Barb is an African-American dyke, unmistakable whether or not she's in heels and a skirt. I am quite sure my aunt has never introduced Barb to Uncle John or Aunt Esther, Uncle Henry or Aunt Lillian as her partner, lover, or girlfriend. Yet Barb is unquestionably family, sitting with my grandfather's immediate relatives near the coffin, openly comforting my aunt. My grandfather was a mechanic in Detroit; his surviving brothers and sisters are Lutheran corn farmers from southern Illinois. Most of them never graduated from high school, still speak German at home, and have voted Republican all their lives. From the perspective of many middle- and upper-class urban folks, they are simple rednecks, clods, hillbillies. Working-class writer and activist Elliott maps out three definitions of the word *redneck*. Its denotation: "A member of the white rural laboring class...."[1] Its connotation: "A person who advocates a provincial, conservative, often bigoted sociopolitical attitude characteristic of a redneck...."[2] And lastly its usage by progressives, including many queers: "1. Any person who is racist, violent, uneducated and stupid (as if they are the same thing), womon-hating, gay-bashing, Christian fundamentalist, etc. 2. Used as a synonym for every type of oppressive belief except classism."[3] Many urban queer folks would take one look at my great aunts and uncles and cast them as over-the-top rednecks and homophobes.

Yet in this extended working-class family, unspoken lesbianism balanced against tacit acceptance means that Barb is family, that Aunt Margaret and she are treated as a couple, and that the overt racism Barb would otherwise experience from these people is muffled. Not ideal, but better than frigid denial, better than polite manners and backhanded snubs, better than middle-class "don't ask, don't tell," which would carefully place Barb into the category marked "friend" and have her sit many pews away from immediate family at her lover's father's funeral.

At the same time, it is a balance easily broken. In Port Orford I would never walk down Main Street holding hands with a woman lover. That simple act would be too much. It is also a balance most readily achieved among family or folks who have known each other for decades. If I moved back and lived down the road from a dyke—closeted or not—who hadn't grown up in Port Orford, whose biological family didn't live in town, who was an "outsider," I would worry about her safety.

It isn't that outside the bounds of this fragile balance these rural white people are any more homophobic than the average urban person. Rather the difference lies in urban anonymity. In Ann Arbor if a group of frat boys yells, "Hey, lezzie!" at me or the man sitting next to me on the bus whispers "queer" and spits at me, I'll defend myself in whatever ways necessary, knowing chances are good that I'll never see these men again, or if I do, they won't remember me. On the other hand, in Port Orford if someone harassed me—the balance somehow broken, some invisible line overstepped, drunken bravado overcoming tacit acceptance—I would know him, maybe work with his wife at the cannery, see his kids playing up the river at Butler Bar, encounter him often enough in the grocery store and post office. He would likewise know where I lived, with whom I lived, what car I drove, and where I worked. This lack of anonymity is a simple fact of rural life, one that I often miss in the city, but in the face of bigotry and violence, anonymity provides a certain level of protection.

If I moved back to Port Orford, the daily realities of isolation would compete with my concerns about safety. Living across the street from the chainsaw shop, I would have to drive an hour to spend an evening at a dyke potluck, three hours to hang out at a women's bookstore or see the latest queer movie, seven hours to go to a l/g/b/t pride march. I don't believe I could live easily and happily that isolated from queer community, nor could I live comfortably while always monitoring the balance, measuring the invisible lines that define safety. My loss of home is about being queer.

Let me return now to *exile*. It is a big word, a hard word. It implies not only loss, but a sense of allegiance and connection—however ambivalent—to the place left behind, an attitude of mourning rather than of good riddance. It also carries with it the sense of being pushed out, compelled to leave. Yes, my loss of home is about being queer, but is it *exile?* To answer that, I need to say another thing about anonymity, isolation, and safety, a messier thing.

Throughout my childhood and young adulthood, my father, along with a number of other adults, severely sexually and physically abused me, tying me up, using fire and knives and brute force on my body. My father, who taught for 30 years at the local high school. My father, whom everyone in town knew and respected, even if they thought he was quirky, odd, prone to forgetfulness and unpredictable anger. He no longer lives there, although some of the other adults who abused me still do. In the years since leaving Port Orford, I have been able to shake my perpetrators' power away from me, spending long periods of time uncovering the memories and working through persistent body-deep terror, grief, and confusion. I've done this work in community, supported by many friends, a few good professionals, and a political framework that places the violence I experienced into a larger context. For much of that time, I could not have returned to Port Orford and been physically safe. I lived a kind of exile, knowing I needed the anonymity of a small city halfway across the country to protect me, a city where no one knew my father, where not a single person had participated either tangentially or centrally in my abuse. Today my safety depends less on anonymity and more on an internal set of resources. Even so, I don't know how I would deal, if I moved back, with seeing a small handful of my perpetrators on a regular basis, being known as Bob's kid everywhere I went. Simply put, my desire for community, for physical safety, for emotional well-being and psychological comfort compelled me to leave. Being a queer is one piece of this loss, this exile; abuse is another.

And class is a third. If *queer* is the easiest and *exile* the hardest, then *class* is the most confusing. The economics in Port Orford are simple: jobs are scarce. The life of a Pacific Northwest fishing and logging town depends on the existence of salmon and trees. When the summer salmon runs dwindle and all the old growth trees are cut, jobs vanish into thin air. It is rumored that fishermen now pay their boat mortgages by running drugs—ferrying marijuana, crack, and cocaine from the freighters many miles out at sea back to the cannery where they are then picked up and driven inland. Loggers pay their bills by brush cutting—gathering various kinds of ferns to sell by the pound to florists—and collecting welfare. What remains is the meager four-month-a-year tourist season and a handful of minimum-wage jobs—pumping gas, cashiering, flipping burgers. The lucky few work for the public school district or own land on which they run milk cows and sheep. In short, if I moved back, I probably wouldn't find work. Not only are jobs scarce, but my CP makes job-hunting even harder. Some jobs, like cashiering or flipping burgers, I simply can't do; I don't have enough manual dexterity. Other jobs, like clerical work that requires a lot of typing, I can do but more slowly than many people. Still other jobs I can do well, but potential employers are reluctant to hire me, confusing disability with inability. And if, miraculously,

I did find work, the paycheck probably wouldn't stretch around food, gas, and rent.

To leap from economic realities to class issues in Port Orford holds no challenge. The people who live in dying rural towns and work minimum- or sub-minimum-wage jobs—not temporarily but day after day for their whole working lives—are working-class and poor people. There are some middle-class people who live in Port Orford: the back-to-the-land artists who grow marijuana for money (or did until the federal crackdown more than a decade ago), the young teachers whose first jobs out of college bring them to Pacific High School, the retirees who have settled near Port Orford, lured to Oregon by cheap land. But these people don't stay long. The artists burn out. The young teachers find better jobs in other, more prosperous towns. The retirees grow older and find they need more services than are available in Curry County. The people who stay are poor and working-class. I left because I didn't want to marry and couldn't cashier at Sentry's Market. I left because I hoped to have money above and beyond the dollars spent on rent and food to buy books and music. I left because I didn't want to be poor and feared I would be if I stayed. I will never move back for the same reasons. My loss of home, my exile, is about class.

~~~

Leaving is a complicated thing. I left with a high school diploma and a scholarship to college, grateful to be leaving, but this is only half the truth. The other half is that everyone around me—my parents, teachers, classmates and friends, the women who cashiered at Sentry's Market, the men who drove logging trucks—assumed I would leave, go to college, and become "successful." No one expected me to marry a week after graduation and move up the road from my parents, to die in a drunk-driving car accident or a high-speed game of chase down Highway 101, to have a baby and drop out of school at 15. A high school diploma and a college scholarship were givens in my life.

This is all about class location, which is where class gets confusing. In Port Orford, my family and I were relatively well off: we always had enough to eat; my father was securely employed at the high school; my mother bragged that she had the only Ph.D. in town. We eventually built a big house of our own. Books filled my childhood. We borrowed them by the arm-load from the public library; we bought them by mail-order from book clubs; we cherished trips to the one bookstore in Coos Bay, a town of 10,000 an hour's drive away. We always had health care. I grew up among people for whom none of these things were givens. On the other hand, we wore hand-me-downs and home-made clothes, for years rented tiny two-bedroom houses, owned one beat-up car, and balanced dental bills against new school shoes. I didn't know that in a middle-class town or neighborhood these things would have marked my family and me as something other than well-off.

Who left and who stayed measured in part the class differences at Pacific High School. My best friend from sixth to twelfth grade was poor. She and I spent high school together in college-prep classes, pouring over pre-calculus problems and biology experiments. We both wanted to go to college, to leave rural Oregon, and yet in our senior year as I filled out college applications, Judy made plans to marry her boyfriend of four years. I know now that her decision arose out of financial desperation—her father had just died, and her family was falling deeper into poverty—but at the time, I thought Judy was copping out. I walked away, glad to be leaving Port Orford behind me. Or so I thought.

Only later did I understand what I lost by leaving. Loss of a daily sustaining connection to a landscape that I still carry with me as home. Loss of a rural, white, working-class culture that values neighbors rather than anonymity, that is both tremendously bigoted—particularly racist—and accepting of local eccentricity, that believes in self-sufficiency and depends on family—big extended families not necessarily created in the mold of the Christian right. Loss of a certain pace of life, a certain easy trust. I didn't know when I left at 17 that I would miss the old cars rusting in every third front yard. Miss the friendly chatting in the grocery store, the bank, the post office. Miss being able to hitchhike home, safe because I knew everyone driving by.

If in leaving, I had simply abandoned a whole set of values, a whole way of being in the world, my loss of home would have been of one sort. And I did leave particular pieces of that culture behind: the virulent racism, the unquestioned destruction of the woods, the desperate lack of economic choices faced by the people who stay. But at the same time, I maintained a strong sense of allegiance to the ingenuity that rebuilds cars year after year from the parts found in front yards; to the neighborliness that had my mother trading sugar for eggs, baked goods for hand-me-down clothes, in an endless cycle of borrowing and lending; to the social ethic that has friends dropping by out of the blue for a smoke and a cup of coffee, to catch up on the gossip or help finish shingling the roof; to a plain-spoken, understated way of being. This allegiance underscores all that I lost when I left rural Oregon.

In leaving, I followed in my parents' footsteps. My father, raised poor on a dirt farm in North Dakota, and my mother, raised working-class in Detroit, both left their families to go to college. Their departures were part of an upward scramble toward the middle class, one that succeeded in some regards and failed in others. They were hugely proud of and grateful for the plenty of food in our house. Books, ideas, and education were their most highly valued possessions. No one could accuse them of being "low class" or "white trash," and yet neither of them has ever become comfortably middle-class. My mother still worries that her crooked teeth and choice of clothes mark her. My father remained rough around the edges, never learning middle-class social graces, always happy jury-rigging whatever was broken, his building projects and hair-brained ideas hanging around forever, piles of scrap collecting in the carport, basement, front yard.

My siblings and I inherited this halfway successful scramble. Our grandparents and great uncles and aunts were farmers, grave-diggers, janitors, mechanics; our parents, teachers; and we were to be professors, lawyers, or doctors. As I try to sort the complexity out, I have to ask, does this upward scramble really work: this endless leaving of home, of deeply embodied culture and community, in search of a mirage called the "American Dream"? Instead of professor, lawyer, or doctor, my brother is a high school teacher, my sister, a low-level administrator, and I, a bookkeeper. Did my parents become middle-class in their scramble? Did my siblings and I?

The answers are not that important except for the betrayal that can creep up behind us, make home under our skins. If we leave, never come back, somehow finding ourselves in the middle class, will we forget—or worse, start mocking—the men who can't read, the women who can make a bag of potatoes and five pounds of Velveeta last nearly forever? Will we train the accents out of our voices so far that we'll wake up one day and not recognize ourselves? And what about the people we leave behind? The last time I saw Judy, her two sons playing hide-and-go-seek nearby, we could find nothing to say to each other, that woman who had been my best—and sometimes only—friend for so many years. How do we deal with the loss? For decades my mother missed living in a big, industrial, working-class city; my father would drive every day to the ocean just to see a long, flat horizon like the one he left behind in North Dakota. My brother has returned to rural Oregon, my sister dreams of leaving Seattle for some small town in the North Cascades, and I entertain fantasies of a rural queer community. Is the upward scramble worth the loss? This question leads me back to being queer, to another, similar question: is queer identity worth the loss?

~~~

Queer identity, at least as I know it, is largely urban. The happening places, events, dialogues, the strong communities, the journals, magazines, bookstores, queer organizing, and queer activism are all city-based. Of course rural lesbian, gay, bi, and trans communities exist, but the people and institutions defining queer identity and culture are urban.

For me, coming into my queer identity and untangling my class location have both been rooted in urban life. In moving to an urban, private, liberal arts college, I found what I needed to come out as a dyke: the anonymity of a city, the support of lesbian-feminist activists, and access to queer culture. In that same move, I also found myself living among middle-class people for the first time. Because in Port Orford my family had always defined itself as middle-class—and in truth we were well-educated people who lived somewhere between the working-class loggers and the middle-class retirees—I believed the class differences I felt in my bones amounted to my being a country bumpkin. I assumed my lack of familiarity with trust funds, new cars, designer clothes, trips to

Paris, and credit cards was the same as my lack of familiarity with city buses, skyscrapers, one-way streets, stop lights, and house keys.

Even now after a decade of urban living, the two are hard to separate. I am remembering the first time I went to OutWrite, a national queer writer's conference. From the moment I walked into the posh Boston hotel where the conference was being held, I gawked, staring unbelievingly at the chandeliers, shiny gold railings, ornate doors, in the same way I used to gawk at twenty-story buildings. Saturday night before the big dance party, to which I couldn't afford to go, I had dinner with an acquaintance and a group of her friends, all white, lesbian writers from New York City. We ate at the hotel restaurant, where I spent too much money on not enough food, served by brown-skinned men who were courteous in spite of our ever-changing party and ever-changing food orders. Jo and her friends were all going to the party after dinner and were dressed accordingly, in black plastic miniskirts and diamond earrings, three-piece suits and gold cufflinks, hair carefully molded and shaved in all the right places. In my blue jeans and faded chamois shirt, I felt conspicuous and embarrassed.

At some point the conversation turned to gossip about queer writers not at the conference. Cathy, an editor for a well-known lesbian press, started in on one of "her" writers, a novelist from rural Oregon. Having heard me talk earlier about growing up there, Cathy turned to me and asked, "When Laura asks me to send stuff to her P.O. box because during the winter rains the mail carrier might not be able to navigate the dirt road to her mailbox, is she serious?" I wanted to laugh, to have some clever retort to slide off my tongue. Instead, I politely explained about dirt roads and months of rain. What this New York femme didn't know about rural living didn't offend me; rather it was the complete urban bias of the evening that did. Was I uncomfortable, feeling conspicuous and embarrassed, because of class or because of urban/rural differences? I can't separate the two.

Experiences like this one have brought me to needing words for my class location. Sometimes I say I'm mixed-class, living somewhere between working-class and middle-class in a borderland rarely, if ever, acknowledged or defined. Other times I feel like a bridge: one foot rooted in the working class, connected by way of familiarity and allegiance; the other resting in the middle class, understanding what I gained, as well as lost, in my parents' upward scramble. I span the distance, able to sit in a posh Boston hotel with well-dressed New York butch and femme dykes and not feel *shame*, only *embarrassment*. Or is it as simple as still feeling like a country hick—with all of its class implications—in the city? In any case, it leaves me feeling queer in the queer community.

Just how urban is the most visible of queer identities, how middle-class, how consumer-oriented? I am remembering Stonewall 25, media shorthand for New York City's celebration of the 25th anniversary of the Stonewall Rebellion. If one were to believe the mainstream media and much of the queer media, it was a defining event of queer identity in the '90s. I didn't go. I can't tolerate New York City: its noise, crowds, grime, heat, concrete, and traffic. I inherited my father's rural fear of cities as big and tall as New York. I've gone to queer pride marches for the last 15 years, but Stonewall 25 was different, a commercial extravaganza of huge proportions. From the reports I heard, the tickets for many of the events cost outrageous amounts of money. Who could afford the benefit dance at $150, the concert at $50, the t-shirt at $25? I know that at the 1993 March on Washington trinkets and souvenirs flourished. Not only could one buy 14 different kinds of t-shirts but also coffee mugs, plastic flags, freedom rings, and posters. I can only assume this proliferation was even more astonishing at Stonewall 25. And sliding-scale prices? They're evidently a thing of the past. Stonewall 25 strikes me not so much as a celebration of a powerful and life-changing uprising of queer people, led by transgendered people of color, by drag queens and butch dykes, fed up with the cops, but as a middle- and upper-class urban party that opened its doors only to those who could afford it.

Why does the money that creates Stonewall 25 and events like it rarely find its way to working-class and poor queers? Why does the money stay urban? What about AIDS prevention programs, l/g/b/t youth services, hate-crime monitoring, queer theater in the mountains of rural Oregon, the cornfields of rural Nebraska, the lowlands· of rural South Carolina? Have we collectively turned our backs on the small towns in Oregon that one by one are passing local anti-gay ordinances? Are we in effect abandoning them to the Oregon Citizens Alliance, the Christian right coalition which spearheaded the outrageously homophobic Proposition 9 in 1992 and which, after losing that vote, has directed its attention toward local initiatives? Will we remember and support Brenda and Wanda Hansen of Camp Sister Spirit, white, rural, working-class lesbians who are building and maintaining lesbian and feminist space in rural Mississippi, when the homophobic violence they face—dead dogs in their mailbox, gunfire at night—no longer makes the headlines?

~~~

In "Rural Organizing: Building Community Across Difference," Suzanne Pharr writes:

> If we cannot do rural organizing around lesbian and gay issues, then rural lesbians and gay men are left with limited options: leaving our roots to live in cities; living fearful invisible lives in our rural communities; or with visibility, becoming marginalized, isolated, and endangered. Not one of these options holds the promise of wholeness or freedom.[4]

If we do choose to engage in rural organizing, to effectively build queer communities and foster queer identity in the backwoods, I want us to follow the lead of rural poor and working-class queers. I want urban activists to take a back seat, to lend their support—financial and otherwise—as rural lesbians and gay men, trans and bisexual people build and strengthen community among themselves. This will be the easy part for urban, middle-class queers to do.

The harder part will be understanding the alliances queers—urban and rural—need to create with straight rural people, the same folks urban people call rednecks, hicks, clods, and bigots. Building and supporting these alliances will entail many different kinds of organizing. At the heart of this work needs to be a struggle against economic injustice, since most people—queer and straight—living in rural communities (with the exception of resort towns and retirement enclaves) are poor and working-class. This means confronting unemployment, inadequate food and housing, unaffordable and inaccessible health care and education—issues queer activists have largely ignored. It is neither easy nor glamorous work, sometimes as simple as lending support to a strike or a family out of work, other times as complex as fighting for health care reform that serves the needs of both rural and queer communities. It will be slow work, creating queer visibility and acceptance by building community among queer people most accustomed to isolation and by finding common cause with the very people cast as the country's biggest, most backward homophobes. But it is exactly this kind of work that will erode rural homophobic violence.

Consider, for example, the eight months I lived at the Women's Encampment for a Future of Peace and Justice in rural New York near the town of Romulus. The violence we faced—as a community of women, mostly lesbians, protesting the existence of the largest U.S. Army nuclear weapons storage site in the world—had several sources. The Army Depot was the primary source of jobs for the people in Romulus, and we were a clear and absolute threat to those jobs. We mouthed the rhetoric of economic conversion but never seriously worked on the problems of economic injustice, never asked the hard question, "What happens to the people who work at the Depot after it closes?" Because we—mostly middle-class, urban activists working within the context of the women's peace movement—never asked the question, much less worked toward an answer, we lived in a community that never stopped being angry at us. That anger most typically came out as homophobic violence. By the very nature of activism, activists encounter anger and resistance all the time, but in Romulus, by not addressing the economic issues, the chances of diffusing the anger and working toward true justice were decreased. In addition, the chances of *dyke* activists living in comfortable co-existence with the people of Romulus were zero.

Alongside the issue of economic injustice was the ever-present fact of our queerness—both perceived and actual. In its first two or three years, thousands of women visited and lived at the Camp, and the homophobic violence they encountered was virulent and, for a while, unrelenting. By the time I lived there, seven years after the Camp's founding, our numbers were smaller, and we had settled into a less volatile but still uneasy co-existence with Romulus. To arrive at this relationship, Peace Camp women had worked hard to build alliances with local people—farmers, business owners, the waitresses at the one restaurant in town. One of these alliances was with Bill, the county sheriff. He and his co-workers had done everything from arresting Peace Camp women to issuing us parade permits to helping diffuse violence directed toward us.

During my time at the Camp, I became Bill's contact, a role which made me quite uncomfortable but one I was willing to fill because I knew that an alliance with him, not as our protector, but as a local whom other locals respected, was important. While other Peace Camp women felt scornful and hostile toward Bill, I developed a cordial working relationship with him. I certainly understood their scorn for a burly, uniformed white man toting a gun, hyper-aware that rural sheriffs, just like their urban counterparts, can easily be the occupiers and destroyers of marginalized communities. But at the same time, Bill had been known on more than one occasion to go knocking on doors, looking for the people who had committed homophobic violence. I knew that maintaining an alliance with him was part of nurturing our rural dyke community. The urban women with whom I lived understood my discomfort and ambivalence about our relationship with the county sheriff but not my willingness to maintain it, to stand out on the porch and talk about the weather, the corn crop, and the Peace Camp with Bill.

I want all of us to listen to Suzanne Pharr's words, because wholeness and freedom need to be at the center of queer identity and activism. If queer activists and communities don't create the "options that hold the promise of wholeness [and] freedom" for all queer people, rural as well as urban, working-class and poor as well as middle- and upper-class, we have failed. And if we fail, those of us who are rural or rural-raised, poor and working-class, even mixed-class, will have to continue to make difficult choices, to measure what our losses are worth.

~~~

My leaving gave me a dyke community but didn't change my class location. Before I left, I was a rural, mixed-class, queer child in a straight, rural, working-class town. Afterwards, I was an urban-transplanted, mixed-class, dyke activist in an urban, mostly middle-class, queer community. Occasionally I simply feel as if I've traded one displacement for another and lost home to boot. Most of the time, however, I know that living openly in relative safety as a queer among queers; living thousands of miles away from the people who raped and tortured me as a child; living in a place where finding work is possible; living with easy access to books and music, movies and concerts, when I can afford them—this is life-blood for me. But I hate the cost, hate the kind of exile I feel.

This displacement, marked by my sense of never quite belonging, has become an ordinary condition in my life, only noticed when I meet new people or travel to new places. Some years ago, a friend and I took a trip to lesbian land in Oregon, visiting Woman-Share, Oregon Women's Land (OWL), and the Healing Ground, hanging out with dykes, hiking in the mountains, splitting fire-wood, planting trees. When we left WomanShare heading north, Janice told us about a dyke-owned natural food store in Myrtle Creek and asked us to say hello to Judith if we stopped. Two hours later we pulled off Interstate 5 into a rickety little logging town. My friend, a Jewish dyke who grew up in suburban Cleveland and suburban Detroit, noticed the John Birch sign tacked under the "Welcome to Myrtle Creek" sign, while I noticed the familiar ram-shackle of Main Street, the hills checkered with overgrown clear-cuts, the one-ton pick-ups with guns resting in their rear windows. We parked and started to make a shopping list: fruit, bread, cheese, munchies for the road. I could feel Marjorie grow uncomfortable and wary, the transition from lesbian land to town, particularly one that advertised its John Birch Society, never easy. On the other hand, I felt alert but comfortable in this place that looked and smelled like home. In white, rural, Christian Oregon, Marjorie's history as an urban, middle-class Jew and mine as a rural, mixed-class gentile measured a chasm between us.

As we walked into the grocery store, the woman at the cash register smiled and said, "Welcome, sisters," and all I could do was smile back. Judith wanted news from WomanShare, asked about Janice and Billie, answered our questions about Eugene, already knew about the woman from Fishpond who had committed suicide a week earlier. News of her death moved quickly through this rural dyke community; as we traveled north, we heard women from southern Oregon to Seattle talking about and grieving for this woman. As I stood in Judith's store, I began to understand that OWL, WomanShare, Rainbow's End, Fly Away Home, Fishpond, and the Healing Ground weren't simply individual, isolated pieces of lesbian land, created and sustained by transient, urban dykes. They are links in a thriving rural, queer network. When Judith asked where I was from, I tried to explain what it meant to discover this network a mere hundred miles east of my unarticulated dyke childhood. I smiled some more as Judith told stories about being a dyke in Myrtle Creek, stories interrupted as she greeted customers by name and exchanged local gossip and news. Marjorie and I left 45 minutes later with a bag of groceries and a pile of stories. As we drove north, I reached out to my ever-present sense of displacement and found it gone for the moment.

I certainly don't believe that I can cure my displacement with a simple move back to the Oregon mountains where I could live at OWL or WomanShare. The questions of safety and paying the rent would still be too big and eventually compel me to leave again. My displacement, my exile, is twined with problems highlighted in the intersection of queer identity, working-class and poor identity, and rural identity, problems that demand not a personal retreat, but long-lasting, systemic changes. The exclusivity of queer community shaped by urban, middle-class assumptions. Economic injustice in the backwoods. The abandonment of rural working-class culture. The pairing of rural people with conservative, oppressive values. The forced choice between rural roots and urban queer life. These problems are the connective tissue that brings the words *queer, class,* and *exile* together. Rather than a relocation back to the Oregon mountains, I want a redistribution of economic resources so that wherever we live—in the backwoods, the suburbs, or the city—there is enough to eat, warm, dry houses for everyone, true universal access to health care and education. I want queer activists to struggle against homophobic violence in rural areas with the same kind of tenacity and creativity we bring to the struggle in urban areas. I want rural queers, working-class queers, poor queers to be leaders in our communities, to shape the ways we will celebrate the 50th anniversary of Stonewall. I want each of us to be able to bring our queerness home.

Clearcut:
Brutes and Bumper
Stickers

The northern spotted owl is a little brown bird that lives in the Pacific Northwest. For years environmentalists and biologists in Oregon have known this bird is in trouble. It is a solitary creature that lives in pairs and nests in old growth forest. Each pair of owls needs a sizeable but disputed number of acres of old growth forest to survive, although the bird may also, depending on which biologists one talks to, live in undisturbed second growth forest. As more and more of its habitat has been cut, the owl has suffered. In 1990 after much pushing by environmentalists, the federal government declared the spotted owl a threatened species, protecting not only the bird under the Endangered Species Act, but also some of the remaining old growth in the Northwest. This move created an uproar, which caught the attention of the national media. All of a sudden, the spotted owl and clearcut logging became a story in *Time Magazine*, on the AP wire, in the *Utne Reader*, on the cover of *Backpacker*, as if this crisis were brand new.

I was already living in Michigan and hungrily read the articles, looked at the photos, recognized the place names. The journalists, both in the mainstream and progressive press, seemed fixated on a certain bumper sticker they found on loggers' pickup trucks. It read, "Save a logger, kill a spotted owl." Depending on the political viewpoint of the journalist and the publication, this favored detail led to one of two analyses. The first focused on unemployment and economic hardship, and the logger became a victim of impending environmental regulations, which would put him out of work. The second scrutinized the big timber companies, their timber management and profiteering; and the logger became an accomplice. Both analyses were easy enough to document, and in both the logger was a brute. As a victim, the logger is a poor dumb brute lashing out—rightly or wrongly—at environmentalists. As an accomplice, he is a loyal brute aiding and abetting the timber industry.

Take for example an article in the *Earth First! Journal*, the newspaper of the radical, in-your-face, direct-action group Earth First!, describing three non-violent blockades of road-building operations and logging sites in British Columbia. The activists involved in the blockades write of the violence and harassment they encountered at the hands of loggers. Throughout the article they use language and images that turn the loggers into dumb brutes. The loggers are described as "Neanderthal thugs" and "club-wielding maniacs," likened to the Ku Klux Klan, and quoted as saying, "People like you are gonna die." To clearly and accurately report unjust, excessive, and frightening violence is one thing; to portray a group of people as dumb brutes is another. An analysis of the loggers' violence follows this description. The activists from the Forest Action Network (FAN) write:

> The anti-environmental movement has been created and funded by the [timber] corporations and FAN holds the corporations responsible for the growing atmosphere of violence and hostility between loggers and environmentalists in British Columbia.... Forest workers [are] indoctrinated to believe that we, in our "quasi-religious zealotry," are trying to take away not only their jobs, but their entire "way of life...." After a decade of layoffs due to increased mechanization and overcutting, the forest industry is playing on its workers' fears about job security and using them to fuel the fires of hostility against us, the new enemy, the dreaded "preservationists."[1]

Their analysis is more articulate than most in outlining corporate responsibility, but the change in language is remarkable. Loggers are no longer Neanderthal thugs but indoctrinated forest workers. FAN wants it all three ways: they want dumb brutes, complicit brutes, and dominating corporate interest. This article is unusual in the environmental press only in that it embraces all three at once.

~~~

Complicit brutes, dumb brutes. I sit at my computer and imagine you, my reader. You have never seen a clearcut, or if you have, you were a tourist. Regardless of what you think about the timber industry, you believe loggers are butchers, maybe even murderers.

Perhaps I'm oversimplifying. Maybe your people are coal miners or oil drillers. Maybe you're a logger or fisherman. Or maybe, like me, you grew up among them. If so, you will understand my need to talk about complicity and stupidity, although our understandings may differ dramatically. Maybe you're intimately involved in Native American land-rights struggles: forced relocation at Big Mountain, fishing rights on the Columbia River, preservation of sacred ground in the Black Hills. If so, you will know white people in general as butchers and murderers. You may get lost in the jargon but understand the politics or vice versa, or you may understand both and wonder why I'm wasting paper. Whomever you are, let me tell you three stories.

~~~

1977. My father and I are building a big wooden house. This summer he and I are framing the walls, putting the siding on, nailing 2x4s together, cutting beams to length. We get our lumber from Tucker's Mill, a one-family sawmill 20 miles north of us. Most of the other mills have closed permanently; the Siskiyou National Forest is nearly logged out. I love the lumber drops. Mr. Tucker comes driving up our logging road driveway in his flatbed truck loaded high with wood. I know the dimensions—1x6, 2x4, 2x6, 2x12, 4x8—by sight, some rough-cut, others planed, the 2x4s and 2x6s stained red on both ends. The wood slides off the flatbed with a crash. After Mr. Tucker leaves, we cut the steel bands that hold the load together and begin to stack the lumber. My hands turn sticky and rough from the pockets of sap oozing from the fresh-cut wood.

Then one day we stop. We don't have the lumber we need. My father grumbles about Mr. Tucker. We need the support beams—the biggest 4 inches thick by 16 inches wide by 24 feet long. They have to be free of heart center, sawed from the strongest part of the log, avoiding the softer core wood that runs down the center of a tree. We wait for two weeks before my father finally calls the mill to complain. Mr. Tucker explains he hasn't been able to find logs big enough or long enough to cut a 4x16, 24 feet long, free of heart center. A week later the beams arrive. Mr. Tucker has obviously found the logs he needed.

Unless you're a carpenter, house builder, architect, logger, mill or lumber yard worker, you probably don't know how big a 4x16 beam, 24 feet long, is or how big the log from which it comes has to be. The trees felled, bucked—delimbed and cut into sections—and milled to make the beams that supported our roof had to be gigantic Douglas firs, undoubtedly old growth cut from small stands of trees on privately owned ranches. My father and I never questioned our need for beams this big. I never truly connected those beams to trees. This is complicity. Now let me tell you about stupidity.

~~~

1991. I am visiting Port Orford for the first time in four years. My sister, a neighbor from up the river, and I bask in the sun at Butler Bar, the river cold and green, the rocks we sit on warm, speckled gray and white. Ian tells us about the environmental battles that his stepfather, Jim, has won in the last number of years. Elk River is now classified a Wild and Scenic River, providing a certain level of protection for its spawning beds. Grassy Knob will remain a roadless wilderness area, protecting thousands of acres of old growth forest. Both have been won though protracted struggle against U.S. Forest Service policy and practice.

I think about Jim, a timber cruiser turned environmentalist. A timber cruiser goes into an area targeted for clearcutting, looks at the lay of the land, estimates the board-foot yield per acre and the costs of building roads, marks trees, and reports back to the Forest Service or the private timber company about feasibility and potential profit. Jim knows the hills well, a mountain man who believes in Bigfoot, a bird watcher who built his house with a chainsaw. He and his family live across the river from the salmon hatchery. To get to their house, they wade the river, take a canoe, or hope the gas-powered cable car is working. Not an easy way of life, but one that certainly suits Jim. The spawning bed at Anvil Creek borders his land. I remember the winter drunk teenagers tried to snag spawning salmon from the creek, an illegal but common source of entertainment, equaled only by shooting seagulls at the local dump. Jim heard the ruckus and appeared with his shotgun, ready to shoot. After that, snaggers left Anvil Creek alone. I ask Ian where Jim is this summer, thinking I'd like to see him. "Oh, in British Columbia, making good money that'll last all year, cruising old growth. He's made too much trouble here. The Forest Service won't give him contracts." The man who fights to save the Siskiyous and the Elk River watershed prepares the slopes in British Columbia for clearcutting.

Jim's work as an environmentalist is that of an insider, a logger whose relationship to trees and fish is complex. They are resources to be used as well as beings to be respected and protected. The ecosystem of an old growth forest is neither the untouchable, romanticized forest of many urban environmentalists nor the limitless raw material of North American corporate greed. For Jim and others like him, the woods provide sanctuary, home, and livelihood. What takes Jim to British Columbia; why is he willing to cruise timber—particularly old growth—in any state, province, or country? The answer is simple: money, food on his table, gas in his truck, so he can be a hermit, a mountain man, and an environmentalist during the long rainy season.

Is Jim the dumb brute you expect a logger to be? Probably not, but you don't like the ambiguity. Or maybe you're feeling tricked. Did you expect a story about a working-class redneck, a faller or choker setter, a bucker or truck driver, or maybe the man who pulls greenchain—pulling the fresh-cut lumber off the saw—at the mill? That's my third story, but these men are no more complicit than the 13-year-old who loved lumber and helped her father build a big wooden house, no more stupid than Jim.

~~~

My mother teaches composition and literature at the community college in Coos Bay, a logging town that almost collapsed when

Weyerhaeuser permanently closed its big mill. Every quarter she teaches out-of-work and injured loggers and mill workers. If these men had their druthers, they'd still be in the woods, but because of work-related disabilities—either permanent or temporary—mill closings, and the depletion of timber, they need to find other ways to put food on their tables. They have spent years working in the forests and mills. Some started as choker setters, working their way up the ladder to become fallers or foremen. The most dangerous and lowest paying job on a logging crew, a choker setter wraps chain around each log as it lies helter-skelter on the slope so it can be dragged up to the loading area. Others drive logging trucks, know how to navigate the steepest, narrowest logging roads carrying tons of logs behind them. Still others have fed logs into the roar of the sawmill, pulled lumber out the other end. They know logs, trees, the lay of the land, chainsaws, and forklifts as well as urban folks know the criss-cross of streets in their neighborhoods. If you want to see a marbled murrelet, a bird—like the spotted owl—in trouble because it's losing habitat to clearcut logging, ask one of them. They'll know where to look, even give you directions if you're lucky.

A few of these loggers and mill workers write about their work to complete assignments my mother gives them. She says some of their essays break her heart, essays written by men who love the woods and the steep hills of the Siskiyous, who fell and buck the trees, and know the tension between their work and their love. They also know that the two aren't diametrically opposed. Their long days outside, the years of trudging up and down impossibly steep hills, chainsaws balanced over shoulders, feed their love. And in turn their joy at the morning fog lifting off the trees, the sound of woodpeckers and gray squirrels, bolsters their willingness to do the dangerous, body-breaking work of logging. Other essays make my mother grind her teeth: pieces about conquest, the analogy between felling a 300-year-old Douglas fir and raping a woman only thinly veiled, both acts to be bragged about. In these essays, trees are jobs, endlessly renewable resources, lumber, and paper; the natural world, a force to be subdued.

All these loggers and mill workers are fighting poverty, struggling to pay the rent, the mortgage, the medical bills on a paycheck that has vanished. There are few unions in the logging business.

The timber corporations all have long histories of union-busting. The last time the mill workers tried to unionize at Weyerhaeuser's Coos Bay mill, the company threatened to pull out completely if organizing efforts didn't stop. The mill workers wouldn't back down, and Weyerhaeuser did in fact shut the mill down for months. In Coos Bay when people can't find timber or fishing jobs, they work the tourist season May through September and earn minimum wage. So these loggers and mill workers enroll at the community college and sit in my mother's classes, maybe hopeful, but more likely consumed by anxiety.

You, my reader, maybe I am imagining you wrong. Rather than believing that loggers are murderers and that logging is rape pure and simple, maybe you place loggers on some sort of pedestal, as the quintessential exploited worker in a capitalist economy. Maybe you believe that logging is ugly but somehow romantic. Make no mistake: there is nothing romantic about logging. It is dangerous work, fraught with hazards that can tear bodies apart. Mr. Rodgers, the father of my best friend in junior high and high school, lost his left arm to a sawmill. Jim Woodward, who lived upriver from us, could barely walk, his back broken in a logging accident years before. In addition to the catastrophic accidents, there is the routine hearing loss, the nerve damage caused by chainsaw vibration, the missing fingers. Nor are loggers romantic, larger-than-life characters. Some of them hate my queer, socialist-anarchist, feminist, tree-loving, fish-loving self, but their hatred isn't unique. They share it with many people in this country.

They are not brutes by virtue of being loggers. Or if they are, then so am I, so is Jim, and so are the journalists who write about the bumper stickers they find on loggers' pickups. Do these journalists ever look for bumper stickers on logging executives' sedans? Do they ever wonder why the sticker "Save a logging exec, kill a spotted owl" doesn't exist? What story would they write if they stumbled across the bumper sticker I ironically imagine, "Save a logger, save the owls, kill a logging exec"?

Clearcut:
End of the Line

I have lived long enough with my current politics in a world that is being ripped asunder, long enough away from the ordinariness of clearcuts and my unquestioned childhood loyalties, to believe clearcut logging is a crime. At the same time, I am still the kid who lived on the edge of a logged-over national forest; I understand the anger behind "Save a logger, kill a spotted owl." Who is going to save the logger? If we as a country are finally deciding, after five centuries of white-led cultural and environmental rampage across North America, to save the spotted owl and fragments of its habitat, then we as a people need to be accountable to the folks who will be unemployed, possibly homeless and hungry, because of that decision. To turn away from this is to act as if loggers and logging communities are more complicit with environmental destruction than the rest of us.

In truth every one of us who is not poor benefits materially from the belief that we live in a country of endlessly renewable resources. We not only benefit, we perpetuate it. Most of us recognize, in this era of recycling, how we consume paper in endless quantities: paper napkins, paper plates, paper towels, toilet paper, newspaper, cardboard and paper packaging, paper bags, copy paper. But do we know the true cost of a sheet of paper, not the mere cents we pay at our local copy center or office supply store, but the real price? Would we be willing to pay 50 cents, a dollar, per sheet? Think about the lumber from which our homes—if we have homes—were built. How many of us know where it came from? If our houses are new, were old houses torn down as they were built? Was the lumber reused or thrown in the dump? Are we prepared to never buy another new piece of wood furniture? If we use fireplaces or woodstoves, can we commit to never cutting another tree down for firewood, to only burning already-downed wood? Think about the salmon we eat, that sought-after delicacy. How much do we pay for the lox on bagels, the salmon steak; how much would we be willing to pay? The point isn't to feel guilty, but rather responsible, to recognize how our out-of-control consumption creates the logic of and need for clearcutting, creates our belief in endlessly renewable resources. In order for trees and salmon to become truly renewable resources again, we will need to consume much less for a long time. The cycle of a Northwest forest, west of the Cascades, from sapling to early successional trees (alder, tan oak) to climax species (fir, cedar, spruce) is measured in centuries. If we value old growth forests and the life they give the planet—value not just timber, but wilderness—we will have to leave the Siskiyous and other clearcut areas alone for many, many years.

A fuller analysis must also include capitalism and free market trade. At the expense of the environment, loggers, and mill workers, Weyerhaeuser and the other big timber corporations have made billions of dollars of profit in the last decades. Today they are making big money by cutting old growth trees as fast as they can and exporting the unprocessed logs to Japan.[1] Their profits are reaped from private land owned by the timber companies and from public land, controlled by state and federal governments.

In this fuller analysis, we must not forget the role of the U.S. Forest Service. In spite of its own rhetoric, the Forest Service's primary mission isn't to protect wilderness, take care of forest lands, maintain campgrounds and hiking trails. Rather it is to line the pockets of the timber industry with even more profit. It has built tens of thousands of miles of road to benefit no one but logging companies, sometimes pouring far more tax dollars into the roads than the timber giants will ever pull out in trees. It routinely bids land out for clearcutting at a loss. In short the federal government subsidizes Weyerhaeuser and Georgia-Pacific, just as it does big business all over the world. Who is complicit and how?

Part of the answer lies inside capitalism, that economic system we've been brainwashed to accept as inevitable, a system that insists upon profit as the supreme value. Working within this framework, logging executives and stockholders in the timber industry, bureaucrats in the Forest Service, are only doing what capitalism expects when they destroy the last of the old growth forest to make a buck. Still, to blame the system without also holding individuals accountable is to leave the system untouched. Complicity follows twin paths, one tracking the course of capitalism and the other tracking the people who sustain and benefit the most from that system. To end environmental destruction, we have to acknowledge who becomes rich and who pays the heaviest price. And then we must make the accrual of wealth based upon that destruction impossible. In short we need to dismantle capitalism and replace it with an economic system which doesn't place profit ahead of people and the planet.

Blame is simpler. Often when middle-class, urban environmentalists start talking about the spotted owl and environmental destruction, loggers get blamed. Like most working-class people doing the dirty work—whether it be oil drilling or coal mining or logging—loggers are easy, accessible symbols. In contrast logging executives, like corporate America in general, spend considerable time, energy, and money on being slippery and less accessible. Middle-class activists so easily forget about the bosses, the rich white men in suits who run the world, when they face the workers, the working-class men in caulk boots and flannel shirts who run the chainsaws.

Loggers' livelihoods are threatened. Many environmentalists skillfully use statistics to argue that overlogging and mechanization dramatically reduced the number of timber jobs ten to twenty years ago. Concurrently they argue that the recent legislation to protect the spotted owl and fragments of old growth forest won't really affect the availability of timber jobs. But in truth, loggers' livelihoods are being threatened. Fifteen or twenty years ago when the jobs in Port Orford dried up, loggers and mill workers moved to Coquille, Bandon, Myrtle Point, or Coos Bay and found other logging and mill jobs. Now when timber jobs dry up in the few towns that still have meager timber economies, there is nowhere to migrate. The people most intimately affected—those running the chainsaws and forklifts—see the end of the line, and so up go the bumper stickers, "Save a logger, kill a spotted owl." Just as loggers are easy, accessible symbols for the anger of middle-class urban environmentalists, so is the spotted owl an easy target for the unemployed or soon-to-be unemployed logger.

At stake are small, rickety logging and fishing towns like Port Orford. Building supplies or fencing material, cars waiting for repair or worn-out appliances, sit in many front yards. The trees on Main Street, mostly scrubby shore pine, grow leaning north, shaped by the southerly storms that beat the town during the rainy season. The buildings all need new paint jobs. Loose signs bang in the wind. At stake is the fabric of a rural, white working-class culture. I never carried a house key; we simply didn't lock our house. No one at the one bank in town ever asked me for identification; all the tellers knew me by name. It is a culture full of racism, a culture that never blinks an eye at the auto repair shop called the Kar Kare Klinic, the KKK for short. A culture that doesn't know the meaning of anonymity. A culture that takes children born out of wedlock, single mothers, and common law marriages for granted.

I remember in second grade when the plywood mill closed for the first time, half my class moved out of town. Those families simply migrated to Bandon, where they found similar work. Fifteen years ago when a salmon season was tight, commercial fishermen knew the next season would more than make up for it. Today there are no logging jobs in Port Orford and no logging jobs in Bandon or anyplace else in southwest Oregon. Today salmon don't run in the hundreds of thousands, and if one believes the persistent rumors, the cannery no longer houses fish but drugs on their way to the cities hundreds of miles inland.

Today Port Orford is a tourist town, a retirement town, and a hippie artist town, barely hanging on. To thrive in its new makeover, Port Orford would need to be fairly accessible to an urban area, have pleasant warm beaches, and attract rich people ready to spend their money. In reality it's a remote backwoods town that people pass through on their way north up Highway 101, not a place where the rich come to vacation and buy funky art. It's a town with wild, rugged, chilly beaches that tourists admire briefly from their cars, not a resort teeming with people dressed for the sand and sun. Its biggest employer is the public school district. The loggers and mill workers have left, gone back to school, or barely squeak by, piecing together odd jobs. The fishermen have left, lost their boats and gone bankrupt, work the drug trade, or struggle by, catching dungeness crab, red snapper, and ling cod. Many people depend heavily on welfare. I don't know what will happen when the so-called welfare reform really takes effect. All the dubious welfare-to-work programs depend on the existence of work. Schoolteachers, ranchers who own land free and clear, and people who retired to southwest Oregon seem relatively unaffected. In short Port Orford is dying and has been for a long time.

This story of slow death and abandonment has repeated itself in many Northwest logging and fishing towns, and the alternatives offered these towns are disgusting. In July, 1994, I heard two reports on National Public Radio about dying logging towns, one about Aberdeen, Washington, and the other about Weed and Crescent City, both in northern California. In Aberdeen, the reporter went to the construction site of a Walmart store, where the reporter's guide went on and on about how this site represented the revitalization of town. In Weed, the reporter explored local reactions to the possibility of building a maximum-security prison nearby. The California state government specifically pushes the placement of new prisons in towns with failing economies as a way of creating new jobs. After the reporter toured Weed, he traveled to Crescent City, a coastal logging and fishing town where one prison has already been built and a second one has been proposed.

Yes, Walmarts exist across the country. But the development of low-paying service jobs in national and multinational chain stores to the inevitable detriment of locally owned businesses will never be the answer to the economic crises in fishing and logging towns. And yes, with the current overcrowding of prisons, the astounding rates of imprisonment, and the "three strikes and you're out" legislation, the government will build more prisons. But maximum security prisons will no more solve the problem than will Walmarts. The business of locking people up is dirty work to the tenth degree, work that no one really wants, and so the government pawns it off on communities that are in no position to say no. Prisons and national chains may in the short term provide some jobs, but in the long term they will not be a force for revitalization.

Rather we should be considering forest and watershed restoration projects, alternative sources of paper and ways of utilizing existing paper and lumber mills, and truly sustainable logging using techniques that don't destroy ecosystems. I don't know how the working-class culture I grew up in will negotiate the changes that must happen in order to save the old growth forests, but after watching Port Orford struggle for 20 years, I do know there isn't one simple answer.

In the meantime, I have a modest proposal. I suggest that environmentalists turn their attention to timber companies and logging executives. Radical, direct-action activists: go plan non-violent, confrontational blockades of Weyerhaeuser's corporate offices. Find out where the CEO lives. Picket his house. Heat his life up. Disrupt board meetings. Monkey wrench logging execs' cars. Demand that all profits made from old growth trees in the last 20 years be returned to a coalition of logging towns to help in their transition away from a timber economy. Organizers and coalition builders: work with loggers and mill workers. Expose unfair and dangerous labor practices. Bring in OSHA. Help build a union. Passionate, committed lobbyists: spearhead legislation that makes exporting logs a crime, that outlaws making a profit off public land and old growth forest. Work the electoral system. Find the working-class politicians-to-be who understand environmental destruction and rural working-class culture, and get them elected. Logging towns: use the blood money from Weyerhaeuser and its ilk to figure out what's next.

~~~

As citizens of the most powerful imperialist, resource-greedy nation in the world, as consumers who have forgotten the meaning of sustainable yield, are we now serious about changing our relationship to the planet and its resources? Are we changing our attitudes toward trees, fish, water, land? Will we transform our assumptions about profit made at the expense of the environment? If so, we need to be equally serious about what happens to the people and towns that arose from the old belief system.

And all the time, we must be conscious of who the "we" is. The ideas, policies, practices, and history that underlie environmental destruction in this country are European and European-American in origin, regardless of who espouses those ideas now. This means that white people who want to save old growth forests, preserve watersheds, maintain biodiversity have a different relationship to the struggle than do people of color: different from Native peoples, whose genocide has been and still is intimately connected to environmental destruction; different from African-Americans and Latinos and Asian-Americans, who, along with Native peoples, often do the dirty work of environmental degradation—whether it be digging uranium, cleaning up toxic waste, drilling for oil, or harvesting pesticide-laden foods—and who often live with the consequences in their backyards.

Towns like Port Orford have their entire histories rooted in the European-American westward conquest of the United States. For a long time even the land was perceived and used as an endless resource. White people killed millions of Native people to claim ownership of this piece of the planet. White men came to the Northwest greedy for resources, looking for good farm land, gold— the goldrush being one of the major resource frenzies of the 19th century—and timber. Additionally they came to convert Native people to Christianity. Rich industrialists latched on to the market for timber, setting up logging camps that were worked by the same men who had come looking for gold and land. Small towns grew up around the logging camps, around the ports and rivers used to transport gold and logs, around the missions and army outposts. They were towns built upon a certain world view about resources, a certain unquestioned greed, a certain racism, a certain set of convictions about Christianity. They wouldn't exist if capitalism hadn't created a gold frenzy, if wood hadn't been in great demand and hugely profitable, if trees hadn't been conceived of as endless raw material. And today these towns still rest upon the same beliefs. If we are serious about protecting the remaining old growth forests, about saving the spotted owl from extinction, then the beliefs, policies, and practices of the United States have to change. We have to be accountable to the towns and people who will be shaken to their roots by these changes.

If we are not serious, then to put the spotted owl on the En-dangered Species list and protect, at least in the short term, a mere fraction of old growth forest, is in truth to pit loggers against the spotted owl. It is to apply a band-aid to a mortal wound. I don't believe that progressive people in this country truly want a band-aid. I know that as the writer who grew up in the Siskiyou Na-tional Forest loving the trees and feeling a kinship with the loggers, as the adult now grappling with old allegiances and new con-sciousness, as the activist of multiple loyalties, I want more—much more—than a band-aid. I want a revolution in the hills and towns, among the trees, I still call home.

Casino:
An Epilogue

1999. When I started writing about clearcut logging five years ago, I had hoped, however naively, that the uproar about the spotted owl and old growth forest might contain the seeds of real change. I didn't expect the fall of capitalism and the rise of a people- and planet-friendly economic system, but I did think we might start protecting forests, acknowledging the bind logging towns find themselves in, and coming to terms with how most of us are complicit in the whole mess. Unfortunately my optimism seems ill-founded. In 50 years we may look back and recognize the spotted owl controversy as a turning point, but for now not much has changed.

The timber companies still defend their practices, some even claiming environmental stewardship over their land, in effect re-writing the language of timber management. The courts have heard dozens of cases, some of which have stopped logging in specific locations, some of which haven't. U.S. District Judge William Dwyer in 1989 declared a logging moratorium on federal land, awaiting a plan to protect the spotted owl, then lifted it in 1994. Each session of Congress since the spotted owl decision has taken aim at gutting the Endangered Species Act. The Wise Use movement has grown bigger and stronger. Either a front for the timber industry or a grassroots effort organized by fed-up loggers, ranchers, and fishermen, it keeps churning out stories of private, individual landowners harmed by big government environmental regulation.

And as for the environmental movement, not a lot has changed there either. The direct-action, radical wing of the movement continues to tree-sit and protest, successfully slowing or stopping logging in crucial roadless areas, although it has had to re-examine some of its strategies, particularly tree spiking, in the wake of an accident which left a mill worker severely injured. Murray Bookchin and other social ecologists remain the sole proponents of a wide-reaching analysis of capitalism, class structure, and environmental destruction.[1] And the movement as a whole seems bent on an idea of preservation that doesn't examine the links among many different kinds of violence and destruction.

At the White House, Bill Clinton has muddled along. Environmentalists welcomed the shift from a Republican to a Democratic administration, even had high hopes for Clinton and Gore. The President came to office promising a country "where we are pro-growth and pro-environment," and a solution to the timber impasse created by Judge Dwyer's moratorium.[2] His solution, arising from the 1993 Forest Summit in Portland, was a compromise that satisfied no one. It did force the Forest Service into doing watershed and ecosystem reviews before making timber sales, significantly transforming policies in some districts. At the same time Option 9, as Clinton's compromise was named, allowed a full third of remaining old growth forest to be cut. Logs were still being exported. Logging practices stayed essentially the same. Timber corporations were still making money hand over fist. And yet Option 9 reduced the timber yield on federal lands significantly enough to create yet more unemployment in logging communities and didn't offer real solutions to the unemployed loggers and mill workers. Then in 1995, Clinton undercut his own compromise, signing into law a rider, written by the Republican leadership in Congress, that basically exempted all federal timber sales from environmental regulation. A year and a half and many old growth logs later, this rider was repealed, leaving the woods to Option 9 again.

In the meantime, the timber industry grows more multinational. Mills shut down in the United States and reappear in Mexico. As timber supplies dwindle in the United States, clearcutting spreads to Russia. And along Elk River, privately owned land is being stripped as fast as possible, second growth "junk" trees cut for paper chip. I haven't been back in years, but my sister tells me that every time she visits another hillside or two or three is bare. She figures that the Marshes and Wagners, the Wilsons and Mayas, simply feel they want as much money as they can get from their land before government regulation descends and tells them, "This you can do. This you can't." Who is asking the hard questions about logging on private land? Are the hills being replanted? Are streams and spawning beds being protected? Have we learned nothing about ecosystems or sustainable yield? In short, not much has truly changed. But let me tell one more story, a story about one thing that has changed.

~~~

The Weyerhaeuser mill in Coos Bay shut its doors for good in the late '80s. A series of gigantic metal buildings, the mill sits along railroad tracks, sandwiched between Highway 101 and the port. At its peak in the '60s and early '70s, Weyerhaeuser ran three shifts, saws buzzing 24 hours a day. Logging trucks roared in with full loads, pulled out empty. Big rafts of logs floated in the bay. White, steam-like smoke poured from the stacks. I never went inside the mill, just watched men enter and leave, hard hats and lunch pails in hand, at shift change. It was nothing like Tucker's Mill: one saw, two forklifts, and Mr. Tucker standing in the yard with my father, shouting to be heard over the roar.

Now the old Weyerhaeuser mill houses a casino owned and run by the Coquille Indian Tribe. Sporting a green logo in the shape of a stylized saw blade, the Mill Resort and Casino offers a typical array of games, live entertainment, food, and accommodations. Now limousines park outside where once only logging trucks, forklifts, and one-ton pickups ventured.

The federal government dissolved the Coquille Indian Tribe in 1954 after a century of genocide and cultural imperialism. In 1961 the last person died who had learned the Coquilles' native language, Miluk, as a child. The traditional ways of fishing on the Coquille River had been forgotten; the rituals of the salmon bake and potlatch no longer practiced; Tupper Rock, a sacred place to the Coquille tribe, destroyed in the building of a jetty; the people decimated by smallpox and alcohol; treaties broken and land stolen. This is the same story of European-American westward expansion and imperialism repeated again and again. From 1954 on, the Coquille people fought the federal dissolution of their tribe, in 1974 starting to work toward restoration, and in 1989 finally becoming a federally recognized tribe again. The rebuilding of their culture has been a slow process marked by a number of firsts: the first salmon bake in many years, the first acquisition of tribal land since the broken treaties and the 1954 termination, the first potlatch in over a century, the first gathering of people to relearn Miluk.

Gaining economic self-sufficiency for the tribe has been one of the goals in this restoration, and the Mill Casino is one of several economic development projects. The Tribe acquired the empty mill in the early '90s and turned it into a gambling palace, complete with neon lights, black jack tables, and slot machines. I have trouble imagining the Mill Casino bustling with a typical Las Vegas crowd, slick upscale tourists mixing with working-class hopefuls on a cheap—or possibly expensive—weekend away. After all, the nearest freeway is two hours away, and the Casino sits, not on a glitzy neon strip or a semi-suburbanized cornfield, but on an industrialized timber port. Instead I picture the guys who used to work for Weyerhaeuser hanging out, drinking beer, playing slots, and reminiscing, sometimes blowing all of next week's grocery money.

Do casinos have anything more substantial to offer logging and fishing towns than do Walmart and maximum-security prisons? Probably not, and yet there is a sorrowful, sweet irony to the Mill Casino. The logging industry collapses under its own weight because trees are not as endless as white people believed. The Coquille people struggle to revitalize a culture and community nearly destroyed by the same forces that declared trees and land and fish commodities in the first place. The white, working-class people left in the wake of Weyerhaeuser and a messy struggle over environmental preservation squeak by, many of them growing desperate, angry, and poorer. Out of the shambles arises a casino. For some white people in Coos Bay, it fuels moral indignation; for others who work the tourist season, it is a cause for hope. And for the Coquille people, maybe it's part of regaining a piece of what they lost in the last 150 years. The Mill Casino is not by any stretch of the imagination the revolutionary solution for which I ache, but it is an irony appropriate to the complexity surrounding clearcut logging.

II: BODIES

Late at night
as I trace the long curve of your body,
tremors touch skin, reach inside,
and I expect to be taunted, only to have you
rise beneath my hands, ask for more.

—from "Tremors"

Freaks and Queers

I: Naming

Handicapped. A disabled person sits on the street, begging for her next meal. This is how we survived in Europe and the United States as cities grew big and the economy moved from a land base to an industrial base. We were beggars, caps in hand. This is how some of us still survive. Seattle, 1989: a white man sits on the sidewalk, leaning against an iron fence. He smells of whiskey and urine, his body wrapped in torn cloth. His legs are toothpick-thin, knees bent inward. Beside him leans a set of crutches. A Styrofoam cup, half full of coins, sits on the sidewalk in front of him. Puget Sound stretches out behind him, water sparkling in the sun. Tourists bustle by. He strains his head up, trying to catch their eyes. Cap in hand. *Handicapped.*[1]

   Disabled. The car stalled in the left lane of traffic is disabled. Or alternatively, the broad stairs curving into a public building disable the man in a wheelchair. That word used as a noun (the *disabled* or people with *disabilities*), an adjective (*disabled* people), a verb (the accident *disabled* her): in all its forms it means "unable," but where does our inability lie? Are our bodies like stalled cars? Or does disability live in the social and physical environment, in the stairs that have no accompanying ramp? I think about language. I often call nondisabled people able-bodied, or, when I'm feeling confrontational, *temporarily* able-bodied. But if I call myself disabled in order to describe how the ableist world treats me as a person with cerebral palsy, then shouldn't I call nondisabled people *enabled*? That word locates the condition of being nondisabled, not in the nondisabled body, but in the world's reaction to that body. This is not a semantic game.

Cripple. The woman who walks with a limp, the kid who uses braces, the man with gnarly hands hear the word *cripple* every day in a hostile nondisabled world. At the same time, we in the disability rights movement create crip culture, tell crip jokes, identify a sensibility we call crip humor. Nancy Mairs writes:

> I am a cripple. I choose this word to name me.... People—crippled or not—wince at the word *cripple*, as they do not at *handicapped* or *disabled*. Perhaps I want them to wince. I want them to see me as a tough customer, one to whom the fates/gods/viruses have not been kind, but who can face the brutal truth of her existence squarely. As a cripple, I swagger.[2]

Gimp. Slang meaning "to limp." *Gimp* comes from the word *gammy*, which hobos in the 18th century used among themselves to describe dangerous or unwelcoming places. Hobo to hobo, passing on the road: "Don't go there. It's gammy." Insider language, hobo solidarity. And now a few centuries later, one disabled person greets another, "Hey, gimp. How ya doin?" Insider language, gimp solidarity.

Retard. I learned early that words can bruise a body. I have been called *retard* too many times, that word sliding off the tongues of doctors, classmates, neighbors, teachers, well-meaning strangers on the street. In the years before my speech became understandable, I was universally assumed to be "mentally retarded." When I started school, the teachers wanted me in the "special education" program. My parents insisted I be given yet another set of diagnostic tests, including an IQ test, and I—being a white kid who lived in a house full of books, ideas, and grammar-school English, being a disabled kid who had finally learned how to talk—scored well. They let me join the "regular" first grade. I worked overtime to prove those test results right. Still I was *retard, monkey, defect* on the playground, in the streets, those words hurled at my body, accompanied by rocks and rubber erasers. Even at home, I heard their echoes. My father told me more than once to stop walking like a *monkey*. My mother often talked about my birth *defect*. Words bruise a body more easily than rocks and rubber erasers.

Differently abled, physically challenged. Nondisabled people, wanting to cushion us from the cruelty of language, invented these euphemisms. In explaining her choice of the word *cripple*, Nancy Mairs writes:

> *Differently abled* ... partakes of the same semantic hopefulness that transformed countries from *undeveloped* to *underdeveloped*, then to *less developed*, and finally *developing* nations. People have continued to starve in those countries during the shift. Some realities do not obey the dictates of language.[3]

Differently abled is simply easier to say, easier to think about than *disabled* or *handicapped* or *crippled*.

Freak. I hold fast to my dictionary, but the definitions slip and slide, tell half stories. I have to stop here. *Freak* forces me to think about naming.

Handicapped, disabled, cripple, gimp, retard, differently abled. I understand my relationship to each of these words. I scoff at *handicapped*, a word I grew up believing my parents had invented specifically to describe me, my parents who were deeply ashamed of my cerebral palsy and desperately wanted to find a cure. I use the word *disabled* as an adjective to name what this ableist world does to us crips and gimps. *Cripple* makes me flinch; it too often accompanied the sticks and stones on my grade school playground, but I love crip humor, the audacity of turning *cripple* into a word of pride. *Gimp* sings a friendly song, full of irony and understanding. *Retard* on the other hand draws blood every time, a sharp, sharp knife. In the world as it should be, maybe disabled people would be *differently abled*: a world where Braille and audio-recorded editions of books and magazines were a matter of course, and hearing people signed ASL; a world where schools were fully integrated, health care, free and unrationed; a world where universal access meant exactly that; a world where disabled people were not locked up at home or in nursing homes, relegated to sheltered employment and paid sweatshop wages. But, in the world as it is, *differently abled, physically challenged* tell a wishful lie.

Handicapped, disabled, cripple, gimp, retard, differently abled, freak.
I need to stop here. *Freak* I don't understand. It unsettles me. I
don't quite like it, can't imagine using it as some politicized disabled people do. Yet I want *freak* to be as easy as the words *queer*
and *cripple.*

Queer, like *cripple,* is an ironic and serious word I use to describe myself and others in my communities. *Queer* speaks volumes
about who I am, my life as a dyke, my relationship to the dominant culture. Because of when I came out—more than a decade after the Stonewall Rebellion—and where—into a highly politicized
urban dyke community—*queer* has always been easy for me. I
adore its defiant external edge, its comfortable internal truth. *Queer*
belongs to me. So does *cripple* for many of the same reasons. *Queer*
and *cripple* are cousins: words to shock, words to infuse with pride
and self-love, words to resist internalized hatred, words to help
forge a politics. They have been gladly chosen—*queer* by many
gay/lesbian/bi/trans people, *cripple,* or *crip,* by many disabled people.

Freak is another story. Unlike *queer* and *crip,* it has not been
widely embraced in my communities.[4] For me *freak* has a hurtful,
scary edge; it takes *queer* and *cripple* one step too far; it doesn't feel
good or liberating.

This profusion of words and their various relationships to
marginalized people and politicized communities fascinates me.
Which words get embraced, which don't, and why? *Queer* but not
pervert. Cripple, and sometimes *freak,* but not *retard.* Like most of
the ugly and demeaning words used to batter and bait marginalized peoples—racist, sexist, classist, ableist, homophobic slurs—*pervert* and *retard* nearly burst with hurt and bitterness, anger and
reminders of self-hatred.[5] I doubt the l/g/b/t community and the
disability community respectively will ever claim those words as
our own. In contrast *crip, queer,* and *freak* have come to sit on a
cusp. For some of us, they carry too much grief. For others, they
can be chosen with glee and pride. *Queer* and *crip* are mine but not
freak, and I want to know why. What is it about that word? What
bitterness, what pain, does it hold that *cripple,* with its connota-
tions of pitiful, broken bodies, and *queer,* with its sweeping defini-

tions of normality and abnormality, do not? I want to unravel *freak*, to pull on the thread called history.

II: Freak Show

The history of freakdom extends far back into western civilization. The court jester, the pet dwarf, the exhibition of humans in Renaissance England, the myths of giants, minotaurs, and monsters all point to this long history, which reached a pinnacle in the mid-1800s to mid-1900s. During that century, freaks were big entertainment and big business. Freak shows populated the United States, and people flocked to the circus, the carnival, the storefront dime museum. They came to gawk at freaks, savages, and geeks. They came to be educated and entertained, titillated and repulsed. They came to have their ideas of normal and abnormal, superior and inferior, their sense of self, confirmed and strengthened. And gawk they did. But who were they gawking at? This is where I want to start.

Whatever these paying customers—*rubes* in circus lingo—believed, they were not staring at freaks of nature. Rather, the freak show tells the story of an elaborate and calculated social construction that utilized performance and fabrication as well as deeply held cultural beliefs. At the center of this construction is the showman, who, using costuming, staging, elaborate fictional histories, marketing, and choreography, turned people from four groups into freaks. First, disabled people, both white people and people of color, became Armless Wonders, Frog Men, Giants, Midgets, Pinheads, Camel Girls, Wild Men of Borneo, and the like. Second, nondisabled people of color—bought, persuaded, forced, and kidnapped to the United States from colonized countries all over the world—became Cannibals and Savages. Third, nondisabled people of color from the United States became Natives from the Exotic Wilds. And fourth, nondisabled people with visible differences—bearded women, fat women, very thin men, people covered with tattoos, intersexed people—became wondrous and horrifying ex-

hibits. Cultural critic and disability theorist Rosemarie Garland
Thomson argues that the differences among these sometimes over-
lapping groups of people melded together:

> Perhaps the freak show's most remarkable effect was to eradicate
> distinctions among a wide variety of bodies, conflating them un-
> der a single sign of the freak-as-other.... [A]ll the bodily charac-
> teristics that seemed different or threatening to the dominant
> order merged into a kind of motley chorus line of physical differ-
> ence on the freak show stage.... [A] nondisabled person of color
> billed as the "Fiji Cannibal" was equivalent to a physically dis-
> abled, Euro-American called the "Legless Wonder."[6]

In the eyes of the rube, the freak show probably was one big melt-
ing pot of differentness and otherness. At the same time, the differences among the various groups of people who worked as freaks
remain important to understanding the freak show in its entirety.
But whatever the differences, all four groups held one thing in
common: nature did not make them into freaks. The freak show
did, carefully constructing an exaggerated divide between "normal"
and Other, sustained in turn by rubes willing to pay good money
to stare.

Hiriam and Barney Davis performed wildly for their audiences, snapping, snarling, talking gibberish from stage. The hand-
bill sold in conjunction with their display described in lengthy,
imagined detail "What We Know About Waino and Plutano, the
Wild Men of Borneo." In reality Hiriam and Barney were white,
developmentally disabled brothers from an immigrant farm family
who lived in Ohio. Their mother, after many offers which she refused, finally sold them to a persistent showman for a wash pan
full of gold and silver. Off-stage Hiriam and Barney were quiet, un-
assuming men. In one photo they stand flanking their manager
Hanford Lyman. Their hair falls past their shoulders; they sport
neatly trimmed goatees; Hiriam folds his hands in front of him;
Barney cocks his hands on his hips; they look mildly and directly
into the camera.

Ann Thompson, a white woman born without arms, posed as
"The Armless Wonder." From stage she signed and sold photographs as souvenirs, writing with her toes sayings like, "So you per-

ceive it's really true, when hands are lacking, toes will do," or more piously, "Indolence and ease are the rust of the mind." In her autobiography, which she hawked along with her photos and trinkets, Ann presented herself as a respectable, religious lady. In one photo, she sits beside her husband and son, all of them wearing formal Victorian clothing.

William Johnson, a developmentally disabled African-American man from New Jersey, became the "What Is It?" the "missing link," the "Monkey Man." He wore hairy ape-like costumes, shaved his head bald except for a little tuft at the very top, and posed in front of a jungle backdrop. The showmen at P.T. Barnum's American Museum in New York City described William as "a most singular animal, which though it has many of the features and characteristics of both the human and the brute, is not, apparently, either, but in appearance, a mixture of both—the connecting link between humanity and brute creation."[7] Although the way in which he came to the freak show is unknown—Barnum may have bought him at a young age and coerced him into performing at first—William died in his 80s at home, a well-liked and happy man, referred to, by his co-workers, as the "dean of freaks."

Charles Stratton, a working-class short person—*dwarf* in medical terminology—from Connecticut worked the freak show as General Tom Thumb. He played the role of a European aristocrat, complete with resplendent suits, a miniature carriage pulled by ponies, and meetings with rich and famous people around the world, becoming in the process a rich man himself. When Charles and Mercy Lavinia Warren Bump, a short woman who also worked the freak show, fell in love and decided to get married, P.T. Barnum set out, in an extravagant example of showmanship, to turn their wedding into a huge media spectacle. He was successful; 2,000 people attended the event, and *The New York Times* ran a full-page story, headlined "Loving Lilliputians." Charles and Mercy played their roles and used the publicity to springboard another European tour.

Two Congolese men and thirteen Congolese women, wearing large, heavy jewelry in their pierced lips, were bought by circus agent Ludwig Bergonnier and shipped from Africa to the United

States. The poster advertising their display in the Ringling Brothers Circus freak show proclaimed them "Genuine Monster-Mouthed Ubangi Savages World's Most Weird Living Humans from Africa's Darkest Depths." The women wore only gunny sack skirts; the men, dressed in loincloths, carried spears. Ubangi was a name randomly pulled off a map of Africa and had no relationship to where these women and men had actually lived.

The Davis brothers, Thompson, Johnson, Stratton, the African men and women did not slide into the world as infant freaks. They were made freaks, socially constructed for the purposes of entertainment and profit. This construction depended not only upon the showmanship of the "freaks" and their managers. It also capitalized on the eagerness of rubes to gawk at freaks and on the ableism and racism which made the transition from disabled person to freak, nondisabled person of color to freak, even possible. Without this pair of oppressive ideologies, the attendant fear and hatred of disabled people and people of color, and the desire to create an Other against whom one could gauge her/his normality, who could ever believe for even one farcical moment that William Johnson was Darwin's missing link; Barney Davis, a wild man from Borneo; Ann Thompson, an armless wonder?

Ann, in that photo of you with your husband and son, you sit on a rug decorated with crosses, a rug you crocheted. The showmen made a big deal of your dexterity. But did you learn to crochet as a freak show stunt? Or did you, like so many women of your time, sew and knit, embroider and crochet, simply as a necessity and a pastime?

Although ableism and racism enter the picture here, the people who worked the freak show did not live as simple victims. Many of the "freaks" themselves—particularly those who were not developmentally disabled or brought to the United States from Africa, Asia, South and Central America, the Pacific islands, and the Caribbean—controlled their own acts and displays, working alongside their managers to shape profitable shows. Many of them made decent livings; some, like Charles Stratton and Mercy Lavinia Warren Bump, even became wealthy. When P.T. Barnum lost all his money in a bad business deal, Stratton came out of semi-retirement and rescued him by agreeing to go on yet another lucrative European tour. Others, like the Hilton sisters, conjoined twins who worked in the mid-1900s, became their own managers, or, like Bump and her Lilliputian Opera Company, formed their own performing groups, which were employed by dime museums and traveling vaudeville companies. In other words, white, nondisabled freak show owners and managers didn't only exploit "their freaks." The two groups also colluded together to dupe the audience, to make a buck off the rube's gullibility. In the subculture of the freak show, rubes became the exploited victims—explicitly lied to, charged outrageous sums for mere trinkets, pickpocketed, or merely given incorrect change at the ticket counter.

Charles, there is a picture of you, taken during a visit with the Queen of England. You have a miniature sword drawn and are staging a fight with a poodle. Your wife, Mercy, writes of embarrassment and outrage. Of presidential candidate Stephen Douglas, she remembers: "He expressed great pleasure at again seeing me, and as I stood before him he took my hand and, drawing me toward him, stooped to kiss me. I instinctively drew back, feeling my face suffused with blushes. It seemed impossible to make people at first understand that I was not a child."[8] *Did you share her embarrassment and outrage as you faced that poodle? Or did you and Barnum laugh long and hard as you concocted your stunts?*

~~~

The questions about exploitation are complicated; simple answers collapse easily. Robert Bogdan in his history *Freak Show* excerpts a letter he received from freak show manager Ward Hall: "I exhibited freaks and exploited them for years. Now you are going to exploit them. The difference between authors and the news media, and the freak show operators is that we paid them." Bogdan comments, "[Hall's] use of the word *exploit* was playful. He does not think he exploited them. He had a business relationship, complete with contract, with his troupe of human oddities. His livelihood depended on them, as theirs did on him. He had no pretensions of doing good...."[9] Although Bogdan chronicles the social construction of freaks in amazing detail and refuses to situate the people who worked the freak shows as passive victims, I believe he is reaching toward a simple answer to the question of exploitation.

Hall's exploitation of people who worked as freaks may not have revolved around ableism and racism. Maybe he wasn't acting out of fear and hatred of disabled people and people of color, out of his internal psychological sense and the external legislated reality of privilege. And then again, maybe he was. But most certainly, like all the people who profited from the freak show, he used ableism and racism to his benefit. At best, this use of oppression by a white, nondisabled businessman is problematic. In his letter, Hall explicitly casts himself as a boss exploiting his workers, placing the freak show within the context of capitalism. Bogdan defends Hall in a backhanded way when he writes: "[Hall] had no pretensions of doing good." But since when do bosses in most profit-making business have real pretensions of doing good by their workers? Doing good may be a byproduct of making profit, but only a byproduct. Is Hall any less exploitative because he was acting as a boss rather than, or in addition to, a racist white person and an ableist nondisabled person?

Any estimation of exploitation in the freak show needs to also include Hall and "his troupe of human oddities" colluding together to exploit the rube. Sometimes this exploitation carried with it a sense of absurdity, a sense that the rubes would believe anything, that they were simple, gullible fools. Other times this exploitation was pure thievery, the sideshow creating situations in which it was easy to steal the rube's money. But to cast the audience only as victim neglects the very real ways in which the freak show bolstered white people's and nondisabled people's sense of superiority and well-being. The social construction of freaks always relied upon the perceived gap between a rube's normality and a freak's abnormality. Unsurprisingly, normality was defined exclusively in terms of whiteness and able-bodiedness.

The complexities of exploitation pile up, layer upon layer. White people and nondisabled people used racism and ableism to turn a profit. The freak show managers and owners were bosses and as such had power over their workers, the people who worked as freaks. Boss and worker together consciously manipulated their audience. That same audience willingly used lies to strengthen its own self-image. Given this maze of relationships, I have trouble accepting the assessment that exploitation in the freak show, if it existed at all, wasn't truly serious. Rather, I believe it exerted influence in many directions.

Working as a freak never meant working in a respectful, liberating environment, but then disabled people had no truly respectful and liberating options available to them in the mid-1800s. They could beg in the streets. They could survive in almshouses, where, as reformer Dorothea Dix put it, mentally ill people and developmentally disabled people lived "in cages, closets, cellars, stalls, pens! Chained, naked, beaten with rods, and lashed into obedience."[10] They could live behind closed doors with their families. Consider William Johnson. As a Black, developmentally disabled man who apparently had no surviving family, he had few options. P.T. Barnum found William's counterpart, the woman displayed as the female "What Is It?," abandoned in an outhouse, covered with shit, left to die. In a world such as this, where the freak show existed alongside the street, the almshouse, the outhouse, William's position as the "dean of freaks" doesn't look so bad.

William, late after the exhibits had closed, the rubes gone home, did you and your friends gather backstage to party, passing a bottle of whiskey round and round? Did you entertain some more, pull out your fiddle and play silly squeaky songs? Or did you sit back and listen to one joke after another until you were breathless with laughter?

In many ways working as a freak was similar to working as a prostitute. Cultural worker and working-class scholar Joanna Kadi writes, "Left-wing working-class analysis ... situates prostitution within the context of capitalism (one more *really* lousy job), celebrates the women who survive, thumbs its nose at the moralistic middle-class attitudes that condemn without understanding, and relays the women's stories and perspectives."[11] This same theoretical and political framework can be used to examine the job of freak. Clearly, working as a freak meant working a lousy job, many times the *only* job available, in a hostile ableist and racist world. Sometimes the job was lousier than others. The African women and men who performed as "Ubangi savages" made a nickel on every photograph they sold, nothing else; whereas their manager, Ludwig Bergonnier, made $1,500 a week renting "his display" to the Ringling Brothers Circus. In contrast, Charles Stratton became rich, owning a horse farm and a yacht. Still others, like William Johnson, found community among the people who worked the freak show.

You who ended up in the history books named only "Ubangi Savages," no names of your own: night after night, you paraded around the circus tent, air sticky against your bare skin, burlap prickly against your covered skin. Did you come to hate Bergonnier?

What did the people who worked as freaks think of their jobs, their lives? I want to hear their stories, but like the stories of other marginalized people, they were most often never told, but rather eaten up, thrown away, lost in the daily grind of survival. Some of the "freaks" didn't read or write, due to their particular disabilities or to the material/social circumstances of their lives. Or, as in the case of many of the people brought here from other countries, they didn't speak English and/or didn't come from cultures that passed stories through the written word. A few "freaks" did write autobiographies, but these pamphlets or books were mostly part of the whole production, sold alongside the handbills and photos. These stories ended up being part of the showmen's hyperbole. So, in order to reconstruct, celebrate, and understand the lives of the people who worked the freak show, I rely on historians, like Robert Bogdan, who have sifted through thousands of handbills, posters, newspaper articles, and promotional garbage used to create The Armless Wonder, The Wild Men of Borneo. In large part, I will never truly know their lives but can only use my imagination, political sensibilities, and intuition to fill the holes between the outrageous headlines in *The New York Times* and other newspapers and the outrageous handbills sold at the carnival.

The historians who moralize about the freak show frustrate me. These academics will take a detail, like the fact that Hiriam and Barney Davis's mother sold her sons to a showman, and use it to demonstrate just how despicable showmen could be and how oppressive the freak show was. The disturbing fact that many of the people who worked as freaks—disabled people from the

United States[12] as well as people from colonized countries—were sold into the business needs to be examined. The question, why were they sold, has to be asked. Certainly, in many cases, the answer must revolve around fear and hatred, undiluted ableism and racism, imperialism and capitalism. But consider Hiriam and Barney. They were sold for a wash pan full of gold and silver. What did that wash pan mean to their mother, Catherine Davis? My sources suggest, although don't explicitly state, that the Davises were a *poor* immigrant farm family. Did that gold and silver mean economic survival to Catherine Davis? What happened to working-class and poor disabled people who needed care but whose families could not provide it? The options did not abound: the almshouse, the street, the freak show. Rather than moralize and condemn, I want freak show historians to examine the whole context, including racism, ableism, and classism, and begin to build a complex understanding of exploitation. Like prostitutes, the people who worked as freaks—especially those who had some control over their own display—grasped an exploitative situation in an exploitative world and, as often as possible, turned it to their benefit.

At the same time, the people who had the least power in the freak show—people from colonized countries and developmentally disabled people—underscore just how exploitative this institution could be. Many of the people of color brought to the United States died bleak deaths of pneumonia, pleurisy, or tuberculosis. They died on the long ship rides. They died wanting desperately to return to their home countries. They did not want to be part of the freak show; they never came to like the freak show; they didn't become showmen and -women in their own right. Instead, the circus, the dime museum, the vaudeville act, the natural history museum were sites of one more atrocity in a long line of imperialist atrocities. Likewise, developmentally disabled people most frequently had no control over their displays. Some lacked the cognitive abilities to say yes or no to their own exhibition; others were simply trapped by unscrupulous managers, who typically were also their legal guardians. Although some developmentally disabled people had what appear to be good and happy relationships with their managers, the dual role of showman and legal guardian is a set-up for exploitation.

The display of both groups of people capitalized on the theory of the time that nondisabled people of color and developmentally disabled people embodied the missing link between primates and humans. Eminent zoologist Baron Georges Cuvier wrote in the early 1800s:

> The negro race is confined to the south of Mount Atlas. Its characteristics are, black complexion, woolly hair, compressed cranium, and flattish nose. In the prominence of the lower part of the face, and the thickness of the lips, it manifestly approaches the monkey tribe.[13]

Much the same was believed about developmentally disabled people. Following the same train of thought as Cuvier, German scientist Carl Vogt wrote in 1867 even more explicitly about evolutionary theory:

> Microcephalics [people with a type of developmental disability medically known as microcephalia] must necessarily represent an earlier developmental state of the human being ... ; they reveal to us one of the milestones which the human passed by during the course of his historical evolution.[14]

The racism and ableism imbedded in these theories intersect intensely in the exhibition of developmentally disabled people of color. Consider the story of two developmentally disabled siblings kidnapped as children from San Salvador. Called "Maximo" and "Bartola," they were declared to be from "a long-lost race of Aztecs." Scientists and anthropologists studied them; showmen displayed them. Both groups helped create and defend the "long-lost race" fabrication, anthropologists to substantiate their theories, showmen to make money, each feeding off the other. They used a variety of observations as their proof. They emphasized physical attributes associated with being disabled by microcephalia, particularly short stature and a slightly sloping skull. They took note of "Maximo's" and "Bartola's" dark skin and thick black hair. They made much of their subjects' language use and food preferences, citing the cultural differences between "civilized" white people and "barbaric" people of color. They exaggerated the specific cognitive abilities/inabilities of "Maximo" and "Bartola." In short, these white, nondisabled men totally intertwined race and disability, racism and ableism, to create "their freaks."

In one set of photos, "Maximo" and "Bartola" are stripped naked, posed against a blank wall. I imagine scientists measuring the diameter of their skulls, the length of their legs, taking notes about their skin color and speech patterns, then snapping these pictures to add to their documentation. A second set of photos has them sitting against a stone wall. "Maximo" wears striped pants and a shirt with a big sun on its front. "Bartola's" dress has a zig-zag design woven through it. Their hair is teased into big, wild afros. "Maximo" looks dazedly beyond the camera; "Bartola" looks down. I imagine showmen carefully arranging their props, calculating their profits. There are no complex or ambiguous answers here to the questions of power, control, and exploitation.

~~~

During the freak show's heyday, today's dominant model of disability—the medical model—did not yet exist. This model defines disability as a personal problem, curable and/or treatable by the medical establishment, which in turn has led to the wholesale medicalization of disabled people. As theorist Michael Oliver puts it:

> Doctors are centrally involved in the lives of disabled people from the determination of whether a foetus is handicapped or not through to the deaths of old people from a variety of disabling conditions. Some of these involvements are, of course, entirely appropriate, as in the diagnosis of impairment, the stabilisation of medical condition after trauma, the treatment of illness occurring independent of disability, and the provision of physical rehabilitation. But doctors are also involved in assessing driving ability, prescribing wheelchairs, determining the allocation of financial benefits, selecting educational provision and measuring work capabilities and potential; in none of these cases is it immediately obvious that medical training and qualifications make doctors the most appropriate persons to be so involved.[15]

In the centuries before medicalization, before the 1930s and '40s when disability became a pathology and the exclusive domain of doctors and hospitals, the Christian western world had encoded disability with many different meanings. Disabled people had sinned. We lacked moral strength. We were the spawn of the devil or the product of god's will. Our bodies/minds reflected events that happened during our mothers' pregnancies.

At the time of the freak show, disabled people were no longer monsters in the minds of nondisabled people, but rather extraordinary creatures, not entirely human, about whom everyone—"professional" people and the general public alike—was curious. Doctors routinely robbed the graves of "giants" in order to measure their skeletons and place them in museums. Scientists described disabled people in terms like "female, belonging to the monocephalic, ileadelphic class of monsters by fusion,"[16] language that came from the "science" of teratology, the centuries-old study of monsters. Anthropologists studied disabled people with an eye toward evolutionary theory. Rubes paid good money to gawk.

Hiriam, did you ever stop mid-performance, stop up there on your dime museum platform and stare back, turning your mild and direct gaze back on the rubes, gawking at the gawkers, entertained by your own audience?

At the same time, there were signs of the move toward medicalization. Many people who worked as freaks were examined by doctors. Often handbills included the testimony of a doctor who verified the "authenticity" of the "freak" and sometimes explained the causes of his or her "freakishness." Tellingly doctors performed this role, rather than anthropologists, priests, or philosophers. But for the century in which the freak show flourished, disability was not yet inextricably linked to pathology, and without pathology, pity and tragedy did not shadow disability to the same extent they do today.

Consequently, the freak show fed upon neither of these, relying instead on voyeurism. The "armless wonder" played the fiddle on stage; the "giant" lived as royalty; the "savage" roared and screamed. These performances didn't create freaks as pitiful or tragic but as curious, odd, surprising, horrifying, wondrous. Freaks were not supercrips. They did not *overcome* disability; they *flaunted* it. Nor were freaks poster children, the modern-day objects of pity, used to raise money on the telethon stage. Instead, the freaks flaunted, and the rubes gawked. In a culture that paired disability and curiosity, voyeurism was morally acceptable. Thus, people flocked without shame or compunction to see the freaks, primed by cultural beliefs about disability to be duped by the lies and fabrications created at the freak show.

In the same way, cultural beliefs about race—notions about the wild savage, the noble savage, and an eagerness to see both—made the exhibition of nondisabled people of color at the freak show and other venues extraordinarily profitable. Take for example the display of Filipino people at the 1904 World's Fair in St. Louis. The exhibit was billed as the "Igorot Village," complete with mostly naked women and men dancing wildly and eating dog stew. One among many "anthropological" displays at the Fair, the Village, as a near perfect representation of the wild savage, attracted by far the most Fair-goers and media attention. Christopher Vaughan in his article "Ogling Igorots" writes:

> The "civilized" Visayans, despite offering hourly theatrical and orchestral performances—concluding with "The Star Spangled Banner," sung in English by the entire village—went relatively ignored in comparison with the Igorots.... Gate receipts at the Igorot concession nearly quadrupled the total for the Visayans and tripled that of the colorful Moros.[17]

It was all too easy for white people to gawk at people of color, using the image of dog-eating savages from far-away "uncivilized" islands both to create and strengthen their sense of white identity and white superiority.

During this same period of time, imperialism had intensified to a fevered pitch, both abroad in places like the Philippines and at home as white people continued to subjugate and destroy Native peoples and cultures. By the time of the 1904 World's Fair, the United States had won the Spanish-American War and gained control over the Philippines. In explaining his decision to solidify the United States' colonial rule there, President McKinley referred to "our civilizing mission." What better way to justify that mission, than to display Filipino people as uncivilized savages?

This interplay between politics and the freak show also oc-
curred on the national level. For instance, the missing-link evolutionary theory, used so profitably by showmen, supported slavery
before Emancipation and the suppression of civil rights after. But
the freak show didn't only *use* this ideology. The display of Black
and white developmentally disabled people and nondisabled people of color as the "missing link" and the "What Is It?" actually
bolstered the theory. The scientists and politicians could point to
William Johnson and say, "See, here is living proof. Look at this
creature." In doing so, they were reaffirming the less-than-human
status of people of color and rationalizing much of their social and
political policy. Simply put, the freak show both fed upon and
gave fuel to imperialism, domestic racist politics, and the cultural
beliefs about wild savages and white superiority.

~~~

The decline of the freak show in the early decades of the 20th century coincided with the medicalization of disability. As pity, tragedy, and medical diagnosis/treatment entered the picture, the
novelty and mystery of disability dissipated. Explicit voyeurism
stopped being socially acceptable except when controlled by the
medical establishment. And later in the 20th century, as colonized
people of color fought back successfully against their colonizers
and as legal segregation in the United States ended and civil rights
started to take hold, the exhibition of people of color also became
unacceptable. Along with these changes came a scorn for the freak
show as an oppressive institution from the bad old days. But I'm
not so sure the freak show is all that dead.

Consider Coco Fusco and Guillermo Gomez-Peña's performance piece "The Couple in the Cage," created in 1992 as part of
the "500 Years of Resistance" celebration.[18] Fusco and Gomez-
Peña costumed themselves in everything from fake leopard skins
to mirrored sunglasses and posed as natives from a newly discovered tribe. They toured natural history museums, art galleries, and
street corners in a cage, performing the script of exotic and noble
savages. In the long tradition of showmen and -women, they even

invented an island in the Gulf of Mexico from which they suppos-
edly came and, as they toured, didn't let on to their ruse. Fusco
and Gomez-Peña expected their audiences to immediately recognize the parody. Instead, as documented in a video shot at the
scene of several performances,[19] many people apparently took the
ruse seriously. Some people expressed shock and disgust. Others,
particularly white people, expounded on their theories about why
Fusco paced back and forth, why Gomez-Peña grunted, staring out
at the audience. Still others paid 50 cents for Polaroid pictures of
the "savages" posed at their bars. Whether these people were serious, whether they all left the performance sites still duped, whether
they truly believed their own theories, is not clear. But at least to
some extent, it appears that "The Couple in the Cage" easily repli-
cated the relationship between rube and freak, suggesting that the
old images of race cultivated by the freak show, rather than being
dead, live astonishingly close to the surface.

The scorn for the freak show also assumes that the bad old
days were really awful, but I'm not so sure that they were in actual-
ity all that bad for some of the "freaks." Listen to the stories
Robert Waldow and Violet and Daisy Hilton tell. All of them lived
during the freak show's decline as medicalization took hold.

Robert Waldow, a tall man born in the 1920s, resisted becoming a giant, a freak. He wanted to be a lawyer, but unable to
get the necessary education, he turned to shoe advertising. And
later, after being pursued for years by showmen, he worked for the
circus, earning a large salary and refusing to participate in the hype
which would have made him appear taller than he really was. At
the same time, doctors also pursued Robert, reporting him to be
the tallest man in the world—this being medical hype, not circus
hype. They refused to leave him alone. In 1936 a Dr. Charles
Humberd showed up uninvited at the Waldow's home. Robert refused a physical exam and wouldn't cooperate with the interview.
Humberd left disgruntled and the next year, unbeknownst to the
Waldows, published an article in the *Journal of the American Medical
Association* called, "Giantism: A Case Study," in which Robert became a case study of a "preacromegalic giant." Because of the article, which cast him as a surly brute, Robert and his family were

deluged with unwelcome attention from the media, the general public, and the medical establishment. In the biography *The Gentleman Giant*, Waldow's father reveals that Robert was far more disturbed and angered by his dealings with doctors than with showmen.

Conjoined twins Daisy and Violet Hilton echo this reaction. These women worked the circus, carnival, and vaudeville circuits from the time they could talk. Early on, their abusive guardians controlled and managed the show. They would lock Daisy and Violet away for days at a time to ensure that no one but rubes paying good money could see them. Later, after a court order freed the sisters, they performed on their own. The cover of one publicity pamphlet has Daisy playing the saxophone, Violet, the piano, and both of them smiling cheerfully at the viewer. Much of their lives they spent fighting poverty as the freak show's popularity waned. And yet in their autobiography, they write about "loath[ing] the very tone of the medical man's voice" and fearing that their guardians would "stop showing us on stage and let the doctors have us—to punch and pinch and take our picture always."[20] Try telling Robert Waldow and the Hilton sisters how oppressive the freak show was, how enlightened the medical model of disability is, how bad the bad old days were. Try telling Coco Fusco and Guillermo Gomez-Peña that the freak show is truly dead.

~~~

The end of the freak show meant the end of a particular kind of employment for the people who had worked as freaks. For nondisabled people of color from the United States, employment by the 1930s didn't hinge heavily on the freak show, and so its decline didn't have a huge impact. And for people from Africa, Asia, South and Central America, the Pacific islands, and the Caribbean, the decline meant only that white people had one less reason to come kidnap and buy people away from their homes. But for disabled people the end of the freak show almost guaranteed unemployment, disability often being codified into law as the inability to work.

In the '30s when Franklin Roosevelt's work programs employed many people, the federal government explicitly deemed disabled people unable to work, stamping their work applications "P.H. Physically handicapped. Substandard. Unemployable," sending them home with small monthly checks. The League of the Physically Handicapped protested in Washington, D.C., occupying the Work Progress Administration's offices, chanting, "We want jobs, not tin cups."[21] In this climate, as freak show jobs disappeared, many disabled people faced a world devoid of employment opportunities.

Listen for instance to Otis Jordan, a disabled African-American man who works the Sutton Sideshow, one of the only remaining freak shows in the country, as "Otis the Frog Man." In 1984, his exhibit was banned from the New York State Fair when someone lodged a complaint about the indignities of displaying disabled people. Otis responded, "Hell, what does she [the woman who made the complaint] want from me—to be on welfare?"[22] Working as a freak may have been a lousy job, but nonetheless it was a job.

III: Pride

Now with this history in hand, can I explain why the word *freak* unsettles me, why I have not embraced this piece of disability history, this story of disabled people who earned their livings by flaunting their disabilities, this heritage of resistance, an in-your-face resistance similar to "We're here, we're queer, get used to it"? Why doesn't the word *freak* connect me easily and directly to subversion? The answer I think lies in the transition from freak show to doctor's office, from curiosity to pity, from entertainment to pathology. The end of the freak show didn't mean the end of our display or the end of voyeurism. We simply traded one kind of freakdom for another.

Take for instance public stripping, the medical practice of stripping disabled children to their underwear and examining them in front of large groups of doctors, medical students, physical therapists, and rehabilitation specialists. They have the child walk back and forth. They squeeze her muscles. They watch his gait, muscle tension, footfall, back curvature. They take notes and talk among themselves about what surgeries and therapies they might recommend. Since the invention of video cameras, they tape the sessions. They justify public stripping by saying it's a training tool for students, a way for a team of professionals to pool knowledge.[23] This isn't a medical practice of decades gone by. As recently as 1996, disability activist Lisa Blumberg reported in *The Disability Rag* that "specialty" clinics (cerebral palsy clinics, spina bifida clinics, muscular dystrophy clinics, etc.) at a variety of teaching hospitals regularly schedule group—rather than private—examinations and conduct surgery screenings in hospital amphitheaters.[24] Excuse me, but isn't public stripping exactly what scientists and anthropologists did to "Maximo" and "Bartola" a century ago? Tell me, what is the difference between the freak show and public stripping? Which is more degrading? Which takes more control away from disabled people? Which lets a large group of nondisabled people gawk unabashedly for free?

Today's freakdom happens in hospitals and doctors' offices. It happens during telethons as people fork over money out of pity, the tragic stories milked until they're dry. It happens in nursing homes where severely disabled people are often forced to live against their wills. It happens on street corners and at bus stops, on playgrounds and in restaurants. It happens when nondisabled people stare, trying to be covert, smacking their children to teach them how to pretend not to stare. A character in the play *P.H.*reaks: The Hidden History of People with Disabilities* juxtaposes the voyeurism of the freak show with the voyeurism of everyday life, saying:

> We're always on display. You think if I walked down the street of your stinking little nowhere town people wouldn't stare at me? Damn right they would, and tell their neighbors and friends and talk about me over dinners and picnics and PTA meetings. Well, if they want to do that, they're going to have to pay me for that privilege. You want to stare at me, fine, it's 25 cents, cash on the barrel. You want a picture, that's another quarter.

My life story. Pay me. You think I'm being exploited? You pay
to go to a baseball game, don't you?[25]

Today's freakdom happens all the time, and we're not even paid
for it. In fact disabled people have, as a group, an astounding unemployment rate of 71 percent.[26] When we do work, we make 64
cents to a nondisabled workers' dollar.[27]

We don't control today's freakdom, unlike the earlier freak
show freakdom, which sometimes we did. The presentation of disability today has been shaped entirely by the medical establishment and the charity industry. That is, until the disability
rights movement came along. This civil rights and liberation movement established Centers for Independent Living all over the country, working to redefine the concept of independence. These
centers offer support and advocacy, helping folks find accessible
housing and personal attendants, funding for adaptive equipment
and job training. Independent living advocates measure independence not by how many tasks one can do without assistance,
but by how much control a disabled person has over his/her life
and by the quality of that life.

The movement founded direct-action, rabble-rousing groups,
like ADAPT[28] and Not Dead Yet,[29] that disrupt nursing home industry conventions, blockade non-accessible public transportation,
occupy the offices of politicians committed to the status quo, and
protest outside courtrooms. Disabled people have a history of direct-action protest, beginning with the League of the Physically
Handicapped's WPA protest. In 1977, disabled people occupied
the HEW (Department of Health, Education, and Welfare) offices
in San Francisco for 25 days, successfully pressuring politicians
into signing Section 504 of the Rehabilitation Act, the first civil
rights legislation in the United States for disabled people.[30] And
today, ADAPT is rabble-rousing hard, both on the streets and in
Congress, to pass a national personal attendant services bill.

The movement is creating a strong, politicized disability culture with a growing body of literature, performances, humor, theory, and political savvy. We have theater, poetry, anthologies,
fiction, magazines, art exhibits, film festivals, analysis and criticism
written by disabled folks, conferences, and a fledgling academic

discipline called Disability Studies. At the same time, there are disabled people working to crossover into mainstream culture, working to become models photographed for the big-name fashion magazines, actors in soap operas and sitcoms and Hollywood movies, recognized artists and writers and journalists.

The movement lobbied hard for laws to end separate and unequal education, for comprehensive civil rights legislation. The 1990 Americans with Disabilities Act (ADA) did not spring from George Bush's head, fully formed and shaped by his goodwill and understanding of disability issues. Rather lawyers schooled in disability rights and disabled White House appointees with a stake in disability politics crafted the bill, disability lobbyists educated and lobbied hard, and grassroots disability activists mobilized to get the ADA passed. In short the disability rights movement, founded in the same storm of social change as women's liberation and gay/lesbian liberation, riding on the energy and framework created by the Black liberation movement, came along and is undoing internalized oppression, making community, creating a culture and sense of identity, and organizing to change the status quo.

These forces are taking freakdom back, declaring that disabled people will be at the center of defining disability, defining our lives, defining who we are and who we want to be. We are declaring that doctors and their pathology, rubes and their money, anthropologists and their theories, gawkers and their so-called innocuous intentions, bullies and their violence, showmen and their hype, Jerry Lewis and his telethon, government bureaucrats and their rules will no longer define us. To arrive as a self-defined people, disabled people, like other marginalized people, need a strong sense of identity. We need to know our history, come to understand which pieces of that history we want to make our own, and develop a self-image full of pride. The women and men who worked the freak show, the freaks who knew how to flaunt their disabilities—the tall man who wore a top hat to add a few inches to his height, the fat woman who refused to diet, the bearded woman who not only refused to shave, but grew her beard longer and longer, the developmentally disabled person who said, "I know

you think I look like an ape. Here let me accentuate that look"—
can certainly teach us a thing or two about identity and pride.

Pride is not an inessential thing. Without pride, disabled people are much more likely to accept unquestioningly the daily material
conditions of ableism: unemployment, poverty, segregated and
substandard education, years spent locked up in nursing homes,
violence perpetrated by caregivers, lack of access. Without pride,
individual and collective resistance to oppression becomes nearly
impossible. But disability pride is no easy thing to come by. Disability
has been soaked in shame, dressed in silence, rooted in isolation.

In 1969 in the backwoods of Oregon, I entered the "regular"
first grade after a long struggle with the school officials who wanted
me in "special education," a battle won only because I had scored
well on an IQ test, my father knew the principal, and the first
grade teacher, who lived upriver from us, liked my family and advocated for me. I became the first disabled kid to be mainstreamed
in the district. Eight years later, the first laws requiring quality public education for disabled kids, the Education for All Handicapped
Children Act and Section 504, were signed. By the mid-1980s,
mainstreaming wasn't a rare occurrence, even in small, rural
schools, but in 1969 I was a first.

No one—neither my family nor my teachers—knew how to
acknowledge and meet my particular disability-related needs while
letting me live a rather ordinary, rough-and-tumble childhood.
They simply had no experience with a smart, gimpy six-year-old
who learned to read quickly but had a hard time with the physical
act of writing, who knew all the answers but whose speech was hard
to understand. In an effort to resolve this tension, everyone ignored
my disability and disability-related needs as much as possible. When
I had trouble handling a glass of water, tying my shoes, picking up
coins, screws, paper clips, writing my name on the blackboard, no
one asked if I needed help. When I couldn't finish an assignment
in the allotted time, teachers insisted I turn it in unfinished. When
my classmates taunted me with *retard, monkey, defect,* no one com-
forted me. I rapidly became the class outcast, and the adults left
me to fend for myself. I took as much distance as I could from the
kids in "special ed." I was determined not to be one of them. I

wanted to be "normal," to pass as nondisabled, even though my shaky hands and slurred speech were impossible to ignore.

Certainly I wasn't the only disabled person I knew. In Port Orford, many of the men had work-related disabilities: missing fingers, arms, and legs, broken backs, serious nerve damage. A good friend of my parents had diabetes. A neighbor girl, seven or eight years younger than me, had CP much like mine. My best friend's brother had severe mental retardation. And yet I knew no one with a disability, none of us willing to talk, each of us hiding as best we could.

No single person underlines this ironic isolation better than Mary Walls, who joined my class in the fourth grade. She wore hearing aids in both ears and split her days between the "regular" and the "special ed" classrooms. We shared a speech therapist. I wish we had grown to be friends, but rather we became enemies, Mary calling me names and me chasing her down. I understand now that Mary lived by trying to read lips, and my lips, because of the way CP affects my speech, are nearly impossible to read. She probably taunted me out of frustration, and I chased her down, as I did none of my other bullies, because I could. I understand now about horizontal hostility: gay men and lesbians disliking bisexual people, transsexual women looking down on drag queens, working-class people fighting with poor people. Marginalized people from many communities create their own internal tensions and hostilities, and disabled people are no exception. I didn't have a disabled friend until I was in my mid-20s, and still today all my close friends, the people I call "chosen family," are nondisabled. Often I feel like an impostor as I write about disability, feel that I'm not disabled enough, not grounded deeply enough in disability community, to put these words on paper. This is the legacy for me of shame, silence, and isolation.

Pride works in direct opposition to internalized oppression. The latter provides fertile ground for shame, denial, self-hatred, and fear. The former encourages anger, strength, and joy. To transform self-hatred into pride is a fundamental act of resistance. In many communities, language becomes one of the arenas for this transformation. Sometimes the words of hatred and violence can be neutralized or even turned into the words of pride. To stare down the bully calling *cripple*, the basher swinging the word *queer* like a baseball bat, to say "Yeah, you're right. I'm queer, I'm a crip. So what?" undercuts the power of those who want us dead.

Many social change movements have used language and naming specifically to create pride and power. In African-American communities, the progression from *Colored* to *Negro* to *Black* both followed and helped give rise to the pride and anger that fueled the Civil Rights Movement. "Black is beautiful" became a powerful rallying cry for Black community and culture. But while the word *Black* so clearly connects itself to pride, the use of the word *nigger* among Black people causes much debate. For some, claiming that word with affection and humor rejects a certain kind of pain and humiliation, but for others, it simply reinforces those same feelings. The ugly words—*faggot, queer, nigger, retard, cripple, freak*—come highly charged with emotional and social history. Which of us can use these words to name our pride? The answer is not logical.

Let me refute even the slightest suggestion that lesbian/gay/bi/trans people who hate the word *queer*, disabled people who hate the words *cripple* and *freak*, Black people who hate the word *nigger* are trapped by their internalized oppression. That would be far too simple and neat. Instead I want to follow a messier course, to examine the ways in which the ugly words we sometimes use to name our pride tap into a complex knot of personal and collective histories. I want to return to my original question: why does the word *freak* unsettle me?

But even as I veer away from the simple and neat argument, the one centered upon the ways oppression can turn around and thrive in the bodies/minds of oppressed people, I must pull my self-hatred out of the bag. Even though the answer to my question about the word *freak* is bigger than self-hatred, I need to stare down the self who wants to be "normal," the kid who thought she could and should pass as nondisabled, the crip still embarrassed by the way her body moves. I can feel slivers of shame, silence, and isolation still imbedded deep in my body. I hate these fragments. In the last decade I've stretched into the joy of being a gimp among gimps, learning anger and subversion, coming to recognize the grace in a gnarly hand, tremor, rolling limp, raspy breath, finding comfort and camaraderie with disabled people. Yet I have not stretched far enough to imagine flaunting my CP, even though flaunting is a tool many disability activists use. They are in effect saying to nondisabled people, "Damn right, you better look. Look long and hard. Watch my crooked hobble, my twitching body, my withered legs. Listen to my hands sign a language you don't even know. Notice my milky eyes I no longer hide behind sunglasses. Look at me straight on, because for all your years of gawking, you've still not seen me." Is flaunting the same as pride? I don't know. But I do know that every time I hear disabled people call themselves freaks, my decades-old self-hatred collides head-on with my relatively new-found pride.

For me *freak* is defined by my personal experience of today's freakdom. Today's freakdom happened to me at Fairview State Hospital in 1965 when the doctors first declared me "retarded." I didn't yet talk and was given an IQ test that relied not on verbal skills, but on fine motor coordination. And I—being a spastic little kid with CP—failed the test miserably. I simply couldn't manipulate their blocks, draw their pictures, or put their puzzles together. Today's freakdom happened every time I was taunted *retard, monkey, weirdo*. It happens every time someone gawks, an occurrence that happens so regularly I rarely even notice. I don't see people—curious, puzzled, anxious—turn their heads to watch my trembling hands, my jerky movements. I don't see people strain to understand me, then decide it's impossible. Long ago I learned to block all those visual intrusions. I only know it happens because my friends notice and tell me. Yet I know I store the gawking in my bones. Today's freakdom happens every time some well-meaning stranger or acquaintance suggests a certain combination of vitamins, crystals, or New Age visualization techniques that she knows will cure my CP. I always want to retort, "Yeah right, like I'm looking for a cure, like my brain cells that died some time before birth will magically regenerate," but the moment inevitably passes before I can even think of the words. This is my personal history of freakdom.

In addition, *freak* is shadowed for me by the complicated collective history of exploitation and subversion at the freak show. I relish the knowledge that there have been people who have taken advantage of white people's and nondisabled people's urge to gawk. I love that disabled people at one time were paid to flaunt and exaggerate their disabilities. At the same time I hate how the freak show reinforced the damaging lies about disabled people and nondisabled people of color. I despise the racism, ableism, capitalism, and imperialism that had showmen buying and kidnapping people into the freak show. I rage at how few choices disabled people had.

To infuse the word *freak* with pride, I would need to step through my personal history of freakdom into the larger collective history of the freak show. Stepping through the last slivers of my self-hatred, through the pain I've paired with gawking and the word *retard*, I could use Charles Stratton's strut, Ann Thompson's turning of the ordinary into the extraordinary, to strengthen my own resistance. I could name myself a freak alongside Daisy Hilton, William Johnson, and Otis Jordan. I want it to work.

Instead the two histories collide in a madcap wheelchair race. My personal history isn't so easy to step through; the slivers tear my skin; the old familiar pain leaves me guarded and cautious. And the collective history is hard to reduce to a pure story of resistance and subversion that I want to celebrate and use. I keep thinking of the people who worked as "Ubangi Savages." Sure, Charles Stratton and Violet Hilton became showmen and -women; they took one set of exploitative conditions they were born into and another set of exploitative conditions associated with their work and subverted them as far as possible. But those African men and women, they were casualties of imperialism; their resistance, reflected in the sheer act of surviving the Ringling Brothers Circus, is not a resistance to celebrate, but one to mourn.

This collision of histories leads me to think about the act of witnessing. Are there kinds of freakdom—public stripping, the unabashed staring on street corners, the exhibition of nondisabled people of color kidnapped to the United States, the display of developmentally disabled people as non-human—that we need to bear witness to rather than incorporate into our pride? How does witness differ from pride? What do they share in common?

~~~

To unravel the relationship of the word *freak* to pride and witness, let me step back for a moment, move to the word *queer*, to the gay/lesbian/bi/trans community. I think it no accident that I've paired the words *queer* and *freak* in this examination of language, pride, and resistance. The ways in which queer people and disabled people experience oppression follow, to a certain extent, parallel paths. Queer identity has been pathologized and medicalized. Until 1973, homosexuality was considered a psychiatric disorder. Today transsexuality and transgenderism, under the names of gender dysphoria and gender identity disorder, are considered psychiatric conditions. Queerness is all too frequently intertwined with shame, silence, and isolation. Queer people, particularly l/g/b/t youth, often live cut off from other queer folk, alone in our schools, neighborhoods, and families of origin. Queer people deal with gawking all the time: when we hold hands in public, defy gender boundaries and norms, insist on recognition for our relationships and families. Intersexed people, transsexuals, and people who don't conform to gender norms—such as bearded women who grow their beards—have their own history at the freak show. Queer people have been told for centuries by church, state, and science that our bodies are abnormal. These parallel paths don't mean that queer folk and disabled folk experience the same oppression; at many points the paths diverge. For example the gawkers often pity crips and beat up queers (although some crips do get beat up, and some queers, pitied). But the places of similarity, the fact that both peoples have been considered freaks of nature, push at the question of pride. How have l/g/b/t people created pride? What are the words and the symbols of that pride?

Queer has accomplished a number of things for the l/g/b/t individuals and communities who have embraced it. The word names a reality. Yes, we are different; we are outsiders; we do not fit the dominant culture's definition of normal. *Queer* celebrates that differentness rather than hiding or denying it. By making *queer* our own, it becomes less a bludgeon. We take a weapon away from the homophobes. *Queer* names a hugely diverse group of people. It brings dykes, faggots, bi's, and trannies in all our variation and difference and overlap under one roof; it is a coalition-building word. For some people the word works; for others it doesn't. The same things can be said of the word *crip* in relationship to the disability community. All of this seems simple enough and is typically as far as the thinking about naming goes.

But I want to push the thinking further. How do people who have lived in shame and isolation create community and pride? How do we even find each other? Let me turn here from the realm of words to the realm of symbol. The pink triangle has been used since the mid-'70s by l/g/b/t people as a symbol to identify ourselves to each other and to the world. The Nazis originally used this symbol during the Holocaust to mark non-Jewish gay men on the streets and in the concentration camps just as the yellow star was used to mark Jews.[31]

The pink triangle functions now as a symbol of identity, witness, and pride in queer communities. As a sign of identity, it communicates both covertly and overtly. That pink triangle graphic worn on a button or stuck on a bumper may not have much meaning to many straight people—particularly those not connected to or aware of queer culture—but among l/g/b/t people, especially in urban centers, it readily signals queer identity to other queer people. In this fashion, the pink triangle functions as an insider's language, a language attempting to include a marginalized people while excluding the oppressor. It is also used more overtly to speak of identity, sometimes incorporated into educational work about the historical oppression of gay people, other times into activist work. As a symbol of witness, it remembers and memorializes the gay men who died in the Holocaust. It keeps the memory of Nazi atrocities alive in our consciousness. It serves as a reminder of the extremity of queer oppression. And as a symbol of pride, the pink triangle neutralizes and transforms hatred, following the same political path as the words *queer, cripple, nigger*. It is worn by out and proud queers. These functions—marking identity, expressing pride, insisting upon witness—go hand in hand, all three important for any marginalized community. In our search for liberation, we can sometimes turn the language and symbols most closely reflecting our oppression into powerful expressions of pride. And yet that equation sometimes betrays history, blurring the difference between witness and pride.

As a symbol of pride, the pink triangle has frequently been divorced from its history. In one ahistorical explanation of this symbol, the owner of a Minneapolis gay bookstore tells his customers that pink triangles represent white gay men/lesbians and black triangles—used by the Nazis to mark social deviants, including, it is assumed, lesbians, during the Holocaust—represent black gay men/lesbians. Divorced from its history, the pink triangle becomes a consumerist symbol, used to sell t-shirts and keychains; it becomes a lie. It is not and never will be the rainbow flag, which Gilbert Baker designed in 1978 specifically as a queer symbol full of unabashed pride and affirmation. To use the rainbow flag is to connect oneself to queer identity and pride as they are currently constructed. To use the pink triangle honestly is to connect oneself to history.

I listen again to my Jewish dyke friends who don't understand the pink triangle as a symbol of pride. They ask me, "Why reclaim this symbol that has meant genocide? My family would never wear yellow stars joyfully as symbols of their pride, perhaps in witness and rage, but never in pride. Why then the pink triangle? How can it possibly be a symbol of pride?" Behind their words, I see the shadows of a collective history, the living reminders of numbers tattooed on forearms, the stories passed down of family and culture destroyed.

Their questions and disbelief ask me to unwind the act of witness from the expression of pride. Both witness and pride strengthen identity, foster resistance, cultivate subversion. People who have lived in shame and isolation need all the pride we can muster, not to mire ourselves in a narrowly defined identity politics, but to sustain broad-based rebellion. And likewise, we need a witness to all our histories, both collective and personal. Yet we also need to remember that witness and pride are not the same. Witness pairs grief and rage with remembrance. Pride pairs joy with a determination to be visible. Witness demands primary adherence to and respect for history. Pride uses history as one of its many tools. Sometimes witness and pride work in concert, other times not. We cannot afford to confuse, merge, blur the two.

~~~

And now I can come back to *freak*. The disabled people who use the word *freak*, are they, like many queer people, betraying witness in their creation of pride? A disabled person who names herself pridefully a freak draws on the history of freakdom and the freak show to strengthen her sense of resistance, to name a truth, to bolster her identity. But in using history this way, is she remembering only Ann Thompson, Violet Hilton, and the developmentally disabled girl who, while on display, took to swearing at the rubes? What about "Maximo" and "Bartola"? What about the nondisabled people of color who died at the freak show, desolate for their homelands? When we name ourselves freaks, are we forgetting the part of history that calls for witness, not pride? Are we blurring the two?

How does the history of the freak show interact with the history of today's freakdom? How do our personal histories enter our collective history? If I had not internalized nondisabled people's gawking to the point that I no longer notice it, if instead I felt pissy and uppity about it, would I be more able to imagine flaunting my CP? Would I be more willing to take the resistance of the people who worked as freaks as my own? Would I gladly use the word to acknowledge a simple truth: that the world considers me a freak?

What about people disabled as adults, people who make it relatively smoothly through the first rounds of denial, grief, and rehab and maybe find the disability rights movement and disability community? They don't have a long personal history of freakdom. Hopefully shame, silence, and isolation haven't been buried deeply in their bodies. What might their relationship to the history of the freak show, to the word *freak*, be? Do they ache toward assimilation, not wanting to approach freakdom? Or does freakdom make immediate sense? I don't know, but their relationships to *freak* probably differ from mine. What about developmentally disabled people? What does *freak* mean to them? Where is the pride in a legacy of being owned by showmen who exhibited you as non-human? Again their relationships to freak show history are bound to differ from mine.

I think of the disabled people I know who call themselves freaks. Many of them are performers, helping to build disability culture and/or working to break into mainstream culture. In using the name *freak*, they claim freak show history both as disabled people and as showmen and -women. They shape pride out of a centuries-old legacy of performing on the street corner, at the open-air fair, in the palace and at the carnival as freak, monster, pet dwarf, court jester, clown. On the other hand, could a disabled person whose personal history included public stripping but not performing as easily break through today's freakdom into that earlier freakdom? The history that for so long has placed us on stage, in front of audiences, sometimes in subversion and resistance, other times in loathing and shame, asks not only for pride, but also for witness as our many different personal histories come tangling into our collective one.

This same profusion of histories exists in other communities. For instance, even though I, along with an entire community of dykes, faggots, bi's, and trannies, have made *queer* mine, the word holds intolerable grief and bitterness for many gay men and lesbians, bisexual and trans people. The effeminate boy who came out in the '50s. The dykes and queens caught in the pre-Stonewall police raids. The trans people with histories that include psychiatric abuse. The folks who can pass as straight and/or normatively gendered and choose do so, who yearn toward true assimilation, an end to differentness. I can't presume to know what relationships each of these people have with the word *queer*. How do their personal histories come crashing into the current, collectively defined use of *queer*? The ugly words follow no logic, sometimes calling out pride, sometimes witness, sometimes both, sometimes neither.

What will feed our pride, that joyful, determined insistence to be recognized both inside and outside ourselves? And what demands witness, our grief-filled, rage-filled remembrance? Which pieces of history, which kinds of humor, which words? Let me return once more to my question, "Why *queer* and *cripple* but not *freak*?" This time I won't expect an answer. Instead, I want to take the image of Barney and Hiriam Davis's mild and direct gaze into the freak show camera and practice that stare when nondisabled people and straight people gawk at me. I want to place Robert Waldow's resistance and Mercy Bump's outrage alongside my lived knowledge that freakdom continues today. I want to remember that whether I call myself *freak* or not, I share much with Ann Thompson and William Johnson, Otis Jordan and Daisy Hilton. I want to refigure the world, insisting that anthropologists never again construct lies like the ones they built around the bodies of "Maximo" and Bartola," that doctors never again publicly strip disabled children. I want to sharpen my pride on what strengthens me, my witness on what haunts me. Whatever we name ourselves, however we end up shattering our self-hatred, shame, silence, and isolation, the goal is the same: to end our daily material oppression.

Reading
Across the Grain

A manual wheelchair sits half in shadow, its large right wheel in a pool of light. The chair is empty, turned 20 degrees away from the camera. The footrests tilt out. The headline above the chair, white letters against black background, reads, "A Business Deal So Good It'll Have People Getting Up And Walking Away." *A public service ad for the Muscular Dystrophy Association.*[1]

~~~

A white woman dressed in black—lace bustier, fishnet stockings, stiletto heels—looks straight at the camera. She gives us a red lipstick smile, blonde hair piled on top of her head, diamond earrings dangling from both ears. She sits sideways across the left wheel of a manual wheelchair, which is turned so its back faces us. *Ellen Stohl on the cover of* New Mobility, *a disability community magazine.*[2]

~~~

Four white people—an old man, an old woman, a younger man, and a little girl—stand in a line facing the camera. The old man folds his hands in front of him. The old woman cocks her right shoulder up high and links her left hand into the crook of the old man's elbow. The younger man takes the old woman's bony hand in his fist. The little girl rolls her head up and to the right, her feet turned to the left, her small hand disappearing into the younger man's bigger one. None of them looks at the camera. The headline in bold serif type declares, "A mental handicap is there for life. So is Mencap." Smaller text in the bottom right hand corner whispers, "Without your help we're handicapped." *An advertising poster for Mencap, a disability charity organization in England.*[3]

~~~

Each of these images tells a story. The empty wheelchair screams
of telethons and the Muscular Dystrophy Association's (MDA)
obsession with finding a cure to the exclusion of supporting independent living and civil rights for disabled people. Ellen Stohl proclaims sexuality, while at the same time uncovering the story of
disabled people objectified, made to be asexual. The Mencap ad
focuses on one of many stories about disability charity, the turning
of disabled people into children. These three stories need telling
separately in all their specific detail. They can also be brought together to tell a single larger story, one about the meaning of images, how those meanings change and shift depending upon the
context, and the many ways in which they enter the body.

Tall, slender, heterosexual, beautiful in the ways the modeling industry defines beauty, and paraplegic, Ellen Stohl provides a
convenient focus for this larger story. Ellen caused a big flap in
1987 when she posed for *Playboy*. That eight-page spread, "Meet
Ellen Stohl,"[4] alternates between text and full-page photos. The
text describes Ellen, her life as a young disabled woman, her attitudes about disability and sexuality. Small, inset photos accom-
pany the words. We see Ellen riding a horse, sitting at her
typewriter, in her wheelchair studying martial arts, smiling in front
of a frat house. These images interest—maybe even titillate—nondisabled viewers because they can't quite believe disabled people
lead regular, everyday lives. The text reads in part: "[Ellen's] a full-
time student, a part-time actress, model, and a public speaker; she
drives a car, rides a horse, skis, studies martial arts—and is con-
fined to a wheelchair."[5] These words thrive on the lies that disability equals passivity, inability, and precludes activities as mundane
as driving a car.

In contrast to the textual emphasis on the many ways in
which Ellen "overcomes" her disability, the big, full-page, soft porn
photos of her contain no visual clues of disability. Her wheelchair
is out of sight in these pictures. They show Ellen half-naked,
breasts in full view, wearing lace and pearls, lying in bed, legs
draped in bedclothes. In one shot she touches the pearls to her
lips. In another she lies back, her right hand reaching under the
sheets, her head turned in posed pleasure. In a third, she looks at

the camera coyly, seductively, smiling a come-hither smile. Ellen caused a big flap.

Many people had opinions about Ellen's appearance in *Playboy*. Some disability activists were pissed because Ellen appeared nondisabled in the most sexualized portion of the spread, this image reinforcing the bitter lie that only nondisabled women are sexual. Others expressed approval, relief, pleasure that disabled women were finally being recognized as sexual beings, regardless of the final presentation of disability or lack thereof. Some feminists railed against *Playboy* and soft pornography, implicitly pitying and judging Ellen even more than they did nondisabled models. Other feminists tried to analyze the contradictory messages, the sexual objectification of women intertwined with the perception of disabled people as asexual, the visual presentation of Ellen as nondisabled contrasted with the textual presentation of her as a supercrip.

This cacophony of opinions overwhelms me. I turn back to the MDA ad, the cover of *New Mobility*, and the Mencap ad. I place the empty wheelchair next to the wheelchair Ellen so easily drapes herself over. I let the images of Ellen and the old woman in the Mencap poster lie side by side. I imagine the American disability charity MDA and the English disability charity Mencap, both posing as saviors of disabled people, duking it out. I watch as Ellen's full-color sexual self stares down Mencap's black-and-white camera.

~~~

The empty wheelchair with its headline, "A Business Deal So Good It'll Have People Getting Up And Walking Away," proclaims that disabled people who use wheelchairs, and by association all disabled people, are simply waiting for the capitalist powers-that-be to find a cure. A cure may exist now or in the future for some disabilities, and may be important in the lives of some disabled people. But by and large we are not waiting to be cured. To frame disability in terms of a cure is to accept the medical model of disability, to think of disabled people as sick, diseased, ill people. Sometimes nondisabled folks ask me what I would do if I could take a magic pill and wake up "normal"—that is, without CP. They always ask in such a way that I know they believe my life to be unbelievably hard. I like telling them that for me having CP is rather like having blue eyes, red hair, and two arms. I don't know my body any other way. The biggest difference is no one gives me grief, denies me employment, treats me as if I were ten years old, because of my blue eyes. My CP simply is not a *medical* condition. I need no specific medical care, medication, or treatment for my CP; the adaptive equipment I use can be found in a computer catalog, not a hospital. Of course, disability comes in many varieties. Some disabled people, depending on their disabilities, may indeed have pressing medical needs for a specific period of time or on an ongoing basis. But having particular medical needs differs from labeling a person with multiple sclerosis as sick, or thinking of quadriplegia as a disease. The disability rights movement, like other social change movements, names systems of oppression as the problem, not individual bodies. In short it is ableism that needs the cure, not our bodies.

Rather than a medical cure, we want civil rights, equal access, gainful employment, the opportunity to live independently, good and respectful health care, unsegregated education. We want to be part of the world, not isolated and shunned. We want a redefinition of values that places disability not on the margins as a dreaded and hated human condition but in the center as a challenge to the dominant culture. Paul Longmore, historian and disability activist, writes:

> [D]eaf and disabled people have been uncovering or formulating sets of alternative values derived from within the deaf and disabled experiences....Those values are markedly different from, and even opposed to, nondisabled majority values. They [disabled people] declare that they prize not self-sufficiency but self-determination, not independence but interdependence, not functional separateness but human community. This values-formation takes disability as its starting point.[6]

Needless to say, a cure is not high on our list of goals.

The MDA, on the other hand, infamous among disability activists for its Labor Day telethon, is hot for a cure. It spends big money on research, but won't buy respirators for those who need them; big money on the next genetic breakthrough, but not on lift bars to make bathrooms accessible. The MDA's telethon fundraises by evoking pity and tragedy, harming disabled people far more than the money helps us. Yes, I know the need for money is huge, and each wheelchair the MDA donates—they do spare a few dollars from research to buy chairs—improves the quality of some disabled person's life. But imagine a group of straight men raking in the bucks for women's rights by portraying women as pitiful and tragic individuals who lead unbearable lives by virtue, not of sexism, but of their femaleness. Or imagine straight people, who purported to advocate for gay/lesbian/bi people, raising money by reaffirming the cultural belief that homosexuality is a devastating but curable condition. These situations would be intolerable; queer and feminist activists would rise up in revolt. But this is exactly where disabled people find ourselves. Nondisabled people, like Jerry Lewis, who purport to be working in the interests of disabled people, turn their backs on disability oppression, rev up the stereotypes of tragic and helpless cripples, and pour the bucks into research rather than civil rights. And disability activists are rising up in revolt, naming the telethon a pity festival and challenging the disability charity industry head on.

Telethons are made worse by a lack of images of disability. If there were plenty of images—disabled people at work and school, disabled people in happy, committed relationships, disabled people as parents and teachers and activists and performers and artists and lawyers and carpenters and nurses—these pity fests would be less of a problem. But that plenty does not yet exist. We cannot turn on our televisions day or night and watch disabled people lead ordinary lives—or at least television's version of ordinary life. Instead, once a year we can watch a string of disabled children and adults parading across our screens, posed as cheerful but tragic poster children, the telethon creating one of the dominant images of disabled people.

Rather than posing for *Playboy*, sexually objectified for an audience of nondisabled, straight men, or playing objectified blonde bombshell for the disability community on the cover of *New Mobility*, Ellen Stohl could be one of those adults appearing on the telethon, objectified by pity, the lights coming on above her, "Pledge your money to help this poor crippled woman." Her wheelchair would become a symbol of tragedy, instead of a tool for mobility, a prop for modeling.

~~~

I look at the three adults and one child in the Mencap poster, all posed to appear as passive children, and I think about the perpetual childhood many disabled people are forced into. I struggle daily against the stereotype of the child-like cripple, having to establish myself over and over again as fully adult in the nondisabled world. All too often my tremoring hands mark me in some inexplicable way as a child. In a society that devalues children, being seen as a child means being patronized, ignored, talked down to. I'd like a nickel for every time I've been patted on the head, called a good little cripple, that message communicated, not necessarily in words, but in body language and a certain tone of voice.

Beyond the stereotypes, there is an actual childhood to which many disabled adults are relegated. Many severely disabled people never leave their parents' homes, are never employed. Or they work in sheltered employment workshops, doing repetitive assembly line tasks, such as sorting nuts and bolts, and are paid by the hour or the piece, either way bringing home only a few dollars a day.[7] Nursing homes, group homes, and the remaining state-run institutions all argue against independent living, repeating over and over that it is their job to protect disabled people.[8] Forced sterilization of developmentally disabled people was a common and legal practice until the mid-1970s. Doctors defended the practice by declaring that people with mental retardation could not be sexually "responsible" and should not be allowed to have children, echoing the eugenics movement of the 1920s.[9] Federal and state regulations can make it difficult for disabled people to marry, have children, and keep them. Say that a disabled man receiving SSI benefits marries a woman who has another source of income. According to current regulations, he might very well lose his benefits, regardless of whether his partner earns enough to support both of them. This situation leads some disabled people to keep their marriages secret.[10] Or as in Michigan in the early '90s, the state can threaten to take away a child from disabled parents, claiming that they cannot adequately care for their baby. In the Michigan case, the parents could not afford child care on their own, and state law forbid their state-funded personal attendants, who helped them with daily-living tasks, from handling their baby. Legally the attendants could help the parents go to the bathroom, for instance, but could not put a diaper on their baby.[11] All these paternalistic forces—legal, medical, financial—create and maintain a real lived childhood for many disabled adults.

Think again about the Labor Day telethon. Some of "Jerry's kids" are 30, 40, 50 years old; they are no longer children, although Jerry Lewis claims them still. If you were to believe Jerry's pitch, you might believe that the children who appear on his pity fest leave his stage to lead tragic lives suspended until MDA finds a cure, rather than growing up to become adults with multi-faceted lives.

By declaring, "A mental handicap is there for life. So is Mencap," Mencap follows in the truest tradition of disability charity, posing as the savior, the white knight in shining armor. These charities first create and exploit the image of disabled people as child-like and then valiantly come to our rescue. Ellen Stohl could, given slightly different circumstances, be the older woman in that Mencap poster, pictured as passive and awkward, child-like without the least hint of sexuality. Instead she poses, fully adult, blatantly sexual, in front of another camera.

~~~

In placing the images of Ellen next to the MDA ad and the Mencap poster, I don't mean to glorify Ellen as she drapes herself over her wheelchair and looks the part of a sex symbol. Rather I want to start a discussion about disability, objectification, and sexuality. Among many marginalized peoples, objectification exoticizes culture, sexualizes bodies, and distorts real lived sexuality: white women as sex things; Asian people as exotic and passive; African-American men as hypersexual, violent predators; working-class and poor women as sluts; gay men as sexually depraved molesters; transsexual people as sexual curiosities and freaks. The list goes on and on. But for disabled people, objectification means something entirely different. To make complete sense of Ellen in the pages of *Playboy*, on the cover of *New Mobility*, this difference needs to be examined.

Consider the pictures of us in medical textbooks. We stand alone and naked against dark backdrops, our "deformities" high-

lighted and notated in the captions, black rectangles positioned in
the images to cover our eyes. The creators of these textbooks
blithely use us to illustrate their texts, while erasing our faces, turning our bodies into inanimate exhibits. While these kinds of medical images are common to many groups of people, they hold,
because of the medical model that frames disability, a particular
power for disabled people. Our bodies are seen so often simply and
entirely as medical conditions. These textbooks objectify us, not
sexualizing the body, but medicalizing it.

Consider telethons. The disabled people up there on stage are
stripped of their real live humanity and become projections, objects to which the audience can attach its pity and beliefs about
tragedy. Telethons are objectification, not exoticizing the body,
but pitying it.

Consider life in a nursing home. Severely disabled people,
most of whom don't need nursing care, are all too often forced into
institutions by a profound lack of resources. When Medicaid
won't pay for personal attendants, when accessible housing can't
be found, when there is no community or family support, nursing
homes become the dumping ground. Journalist Joseph Shapiro
tells this story about Jeff Gunderson, a young disabled man with CP:

> The two nursing homes where Gunderson lived were set up to
> care for the elderly, not the young. Gunderson was required to
> follow the same regime as the generally sickly, elderly people
> around him. This made it easier for the nursing home staff. He
> went to bed at 7 p.m., the same time as his first roommate, a man
> in his eighties. His food was bland, unseasoned, often a form of
> gruel made for the older residents who could not eat solid food....
> Sometimes aides tied him to his bed. They would drag him into
> cold showers as punishment. To make him use the bathroom on
> a schedule convenient for the nurses, they would put ice cubes
> down his pants.... On several occasions, Gunderson says he was
> given a suppository before sleep, and, since he could not move
> by himself, he would spend the night lying in his own feces.[12]

Jeff's experience, while possibly not the norm for nursing homes, is
all too common. I've heard stories of people tied to their wheelchairs, left for hours, stories of untreated bedsores and cockroach-
infested beds, stories of years lived in brain-numbing boredom,

disabled people becoming objects, not sexual or exotic objects, but objects to be passively neglected and actively abused.

Objectification plays many roles in the lives of disabled people, none of which sexualize us. In fact, medicalization, pity, and neglect do exactly the opposite. Consequently, disabled people's relationship to sexual objectification is often complex. A friend once told me: *When I was in high school, I'd go cruising with my girl friends. The boys would hoot and holler at us,* Hey baby, you're hot, *or just wolf whistle. But later if they saw my leg braces and crutches, they'd come over to me, quietly apologize, tell me they didn't mean it. They were sincere. Now 20 years later, now that I'm a dyke, I'm hungry for sexual attention. I want dykes to wolf whistle at me, to stare at my body, not as though I were a freak in a freak show, but stare, eyes full of desire, eyes undressing me. I want them to still mean it after they see my wheelchair.* After my friend told me this story, we simply laughed, unable to put words to our mutual understanding of a complicated twining of escape and loss we both feel.

Sexual objectification is not simple. From one angle, it runs counter to human liberation, enforcing and maintaining institutionalized power differences: women becoming mere sex objects for men's enjoyment, white people exoticizing the bodies and cultures of people of color, rich and middle-class people projecting sexual "irresponsibility" and "promiscuity" onto poor and working-class people. These power imbalances have huge ramifications in people's personal lives and on public policy.

From another angle, sexual objectification is totally intertwined with sexuality. How are our sexual desires expressed and represented? What are the differences between wanted and unwanted sexual gaze? When does that gaze define our sexualities for us, many times in degrading and humiliating ways? And when does that gaze help us create ourselves as sexual beings? These questions lead me to think about sexual objectification, the creation of self-defined sexuality, and the possible intersection of the two. Within a particular community, where images are produced by and for members of that community, can sexual objectification support our real lived sexualities? Lesbian sex artist Persimmon Blackbridge writes:

Pornography is assumed to be made by men and for men. Sexual images by women and for women are never mentioned. It's such a familiar erasure of our lives.... A *Penthouse* portrayal of a woman in bondage and a woman's portrayal of herself in bondage are seen as the same thing. [From this perspective] there is no difference between a tired old view of the Subordinated Other, and a vulnerable self-exploration.[13]

Does the meaning of sexual objectification change depending on context, and if so, how? Is a lesbian strip show at a dyke bar, a drag queen extravaganza at a queer bar, about sexual objectification? Or are they about creating ourselves as sexual subjects? Where is the line between being a sexual object and sexual subject? Does the location of that line change depending on context, community, culture, intent? Can one find herself as a sexual subject through sexual objectification? These are not trivial questions. The feminist sex wars of the 1980s, pitting anti-pornography activists against anti-censorship activists, "pro-sex" feminists against "anti-violence" feminists, were fought over them, and they have no real answers, except in the acknowledgment of complexity.

We all live in a world that both hates sex and is saturated with sex, sex plastered everywhere: television, movies, billboards, magazines, the nightly news. Yet disabled people find no trace of our sexualities in that world. We are genderless, asexual undesirables. This is not an exaggeration. Think first about gender and how perceptions of gender are shaped. To be female and disabled is to be seen as not quite a woman; to be male and disabled, as not quite a man. The mannerisms that help define gender—the ways in which people walk, swing their hips, gesture with their hands, move their mouths and eyes as they talk, take up space with their bodies—are all based upon how nondisabled people move. A woman who walks with crutches does not walk like a "woman"; a man who uses a wheelchair and a ventilator does not move like a "man." The construction of gender depends not only upon the male body and female body, but also upon the nondisabled body.

Now think about sexuality. Disability activist Connie Panzarino writes in her memoir *The Me in the Mirror* about going to a lesbian bar:

...[N]o one would talk to me. Several women at the bar asked my attendant why she brought her "patient" to this kind of place. My attendants explained that I was there because I was a lesbian and they were there because they were working for me.[14]

Or consider the uproar when Los Angeles television news anchor Bree Walker Lampley, who has an inheritable disability that partially fuses bones in the fingers and toes, became pregnant. She was raked over the coals on talk radio for choosing to have a child who might be disabled. Jane Norris, the radio show host, said:

Face the facts here, having that sort of deformity is a strike against you in life. People judge you by your appearance, by the shape of your hands, and the shape of your body and the shape of your face. They just do. They make value judgments about you. Whether it's right or whether it's wrong, it just is.... It would be difficult to bring myself to morally cast my child forever to disfigured hands.[15]

The people who called in to the show reflected Norris's attitude with even more vehemence. One caller said, "I want to know what her motive is for having this child.... Actually, I think it's kind of irresponsible."[16] The step from saying it's morally wrong for a disabled woman to be pregnant to saying it's morally wrong for her to be sexual at all is tiny.[17] Connie is a medical patient, not just another dyke at a dyke bar; Bree is immoral and irresponsible, not just another expectant mother. It is no exaggeration to say that we are genderless, asexual undesirables. We hear and see and feel this at every turn. It digs into our bodies. From this vantage point, sexual objectification appears to be a positive recognition of sexuality.

How do I explain the complicated twining of escape and loss that my friend's story points to? On the one hand, disabled people mostly escape the sexual objectification and harassment many nondisabled women face every day at their jobs and on the streets. It is an escape that has given me a bit of space. Amidst all the staring I absorb and deflect, I am grateful not to have to deal with sexual leering. On the other hand in the absence of sexual gaze of any kind directed at us—wanted or unwanted—we lose ourselves as sexual beings. I almost don't have words for what this absence, this loss, means in my life. It has been a gaping hole, a desolate fog, and a "normal" everyday fact. It has translated into an inability to conceive of myself as attractive and desirable, has added to my sense of being ugly and clumsy. I hate these meanings. In the world as I want it to be, no peoples would be subjected to unwanted sexual gaze. We could all choose ourselves as sexual subjects, sexual objects, sexual beings. There would be a million ways to acknowledge our own and each other's sexualities, none of them connected to oppression. But in the world as it is, sexual objectification is a powerful marker, however damaging, of sexuality. In turn, its absence is also powerful.

~~~

When nondisabled feminists started criticizing Ellen and the disability activists who supported her, I wanted to rant. I am well-schooled in the feminist argument they were making. Most frequently grounded in a white, middle-class, single-issue version of feminism, this argument takes on the generic objectification of women, meaning middle- and upper-class, white, heterosexual, nondisabled women. It ignores the matrix of class, race, sexual orientation, gender, and disability and places gender—or at least a simplified version of gender that ignores transsexuality and transgendered experience—at the absolute center. It goes like this: images of women from advertising to movies to pornography treat women as sexual objects. In turn, objectification helps create and maintain a culture where sexual and physical violence against women is acceptable and permitted, glorified, and romanticized.

This analysis has led to much powerful feminist activism in the past 25 years against rape and child abuse, against pornography and other media portrayals of women. But when taken to its extreme—sometimes in the form of legislation—it has also led to pro-censorship stands, bizarre agreements with the right wing, and narrow, dogmatic views about sex and sexual imagery. It succeeded in bringing to the foreground what is degrading, humiliating, and dangerous about sexual objectification but failed to understand the complicated relationship between the self as subject and the self as object. It spoke eloquently about the damage that can be caused by pornographic sexual representation but failed to embrace the need for pleasure. It named certain sexual behaviors as oppressive, but failed to take into account the multi-layered reality of erotic power.

These failings provided fuel for the conflicts over censorship, the uses of erotica/pornography, and the role of sexual objectification. Unfortunately the feminist sex wars, as the conflicts have been dubbed, didn't result in a new framework, a deeper understanding of sexual objectification, representation, damage, and pleasure, but in a polarization where one is either perceived as anti-porn, pro-censorship, and anti-sex or as pro-porn, anti-censorship, and pro-sex. As I write this, I can almost hear my readers trying to peg me. Which side am I on? Can I be both anti-hate literature—and I believe some pornography falls into that category—and anti-censorship? Critical of sexual objectification and aware of its complexities? Fiercely aware of sexual violence and damage on one hand and sexual pleasure and presence on the other? Can I make enough space to add disability to the discussion?

Many of the feminists who criticized Ellen didn't know two cents about disability and ableism. For them objectification meant only sexual objectification. Within their analytic framework, soft pornography, like *Playboy*, was simply and entirely problematic. They rejected Ellen and the disability activists who supported her as dupes of the patriarchy. I wanted to shake them out of their narrow, single-issue analysis. I won't deny that Ellen is sexually objectified in the pages of *Playboy* and on the cover of *New Mobility*. But within the context of disability, the meaning of this objectification shifts. Ellen becoming a sex object, being seen and acknowledged as sexy, splashed in color across the pages of a sex magazine, represents an important fault line, a sudden and welcome admission of disabled people—or at least one white, heterosexual, disabled woman whose disability can be made invisible before a camera—as sexual.

I look again at Ellen draped over her wheelchair, Ellen dressed to display her ample cleavage and long legs. The photo reminds me of the Ford and GM ads where scantily dressed white women drape themselves over cars and trucks. I remember learning how to pick apart advertisements, to recognize what the capitalist, sexist, racist money-mongers really mean to sell. I place the two images side-by-side—the *New Mobility* cover next to the Ford

ad—and feel compelled to ask a rhetorical question. Can't you recognize the difference? The answer is entirely about context.

~~~

When a people's collective history includes dehumanizing medical
textbook photographs, forced sterilization, pity fests masquerading
as charity, and an asexuality so deeply ingrained in our bodies and
institutionalized in the world that it feels impossible to shake, Ellen's bare skin looks great. But the disability activists who uncondi-
tionally supported Ellen when she posed in *Playboy* also frustrate
me. That eight-page soft porn spread represents an important fault
line, or the beginning of one. At the same time, I want to remind
Ellen's disabled supporters about the dangers of accepting beauty
and sexuality as defined exclusively by nondisabled people, by
straight people, by white people, by rich people, by men. Let us remember disabled bodies in all their variety. I look at my body set
off-center by CP, tense and shaky; my butch body often taken to
be male; my body marked, both visibly and not, by rape. I will
never look like Ellen Stohl. Nor will most of us. We will never, as
Ellen so gracefully does, meet the dominant culture's standards for
beauty and sexual attractiveness. Even if we did, I do not want
Playboy to define anyone's sexuality—female or male, disabled or not.
I believe disability activists need to feel some ambivalence about
Ellen in *Playboy*, even about Ellen on the cover of *New Mobility*.

Anne Finger articulates this exact ambivalence well in an article about a series of ads in *Vogue*. Showcasing extremely expensive
clothes, they center upon a model with no visible disability. She is
dressed in black, wears four-inch heels, and uses, in successive ads,
a wheelchair, a cane, and crutches. In the final photo, one of her
legs appears to have been amputated and placed next to her. Finger analyzes these images, weaving her political sensibilities as a
feminist and disability rights activist together with her personal
struggle as a disabled woman to "feel comfortable with having a
sensual presence in the world."[18] She ends the article, wrapping her
analysis in ambivalence:

> Certainly, the pictures can be quite legitimately read as making a
> joke about disability, of sexualizing disability within nondisabled
> norms (as a kink, acceptable so long as the woman doesn't actu-

ally look as if she needs the paraphernalia). But there's also another movement at work within the photographs: of disability being seen outside the contexts of tragedy and asexuality. Of course, and unfortunately, it happens within the context of feminine sexuality being linked to helplessness, wealth, and a standard of looks that only a very few women, disabled or nondisabled, can be part of. While criticizing what in the layout surely needs to be criticized, we can also see the seed of a positive movement: a seed that will come to fruition when disabled women are able not to be passive objects of art, but to create our own representations—and get them seen and recognized.[19]

I'm saddened that because there are so few images of disabled people, of us as sexual beings, we turn—however ambivalently—to *Playboy* and *Vogue*, as if *Playboy* publisher Hugh Hefner or *Vogue* photographer Helmut Newton could ever do justice to crip sexuality.

In writing about the lack of lesbian images made by lesbians, Susan Stewart of the lesbian sex art collective Kiss and Tell frames ambivalence this way:

Images of lesbians created by lesbians are extremely rare and difficult to find, yet photographs taken by men, of women staged to look like lesbians, are common fair in both porno mags and videos. Lesbians aren't fooled by these images. We know who they are meant for and sometimes they disgust and sadden us and sometimes we are turned on by them. When there is a prolonged drought you tend to get less fussy about the purity of the water you drink... It is all part of what some theorists call "reading across the grain." Some of us have been reading across the grain for so long that our eyes have splinters.[20]

I say *Playboy*'s "Meet Ellen Stohl" and *Vogue*'s advertisements create some mighty big splinters for disabled people.

The answer of course, as Finger suggests, is to create more representations of disabled people. Within disability communities and in mainstream culture, we need images—honest, solid, shimmering, powerful, joyful images—of crip bodies and sexuality in the same way we need crip humor, crip pride, crip culture. We need more short stories like Finger's "Helen and Frida," where Helen Keller and Frida Kahlo, "the two female icons of disability," meet, spend a highly charged afternoon, and end in a deeply pas-

sionate and exploratory kiss.[21] We need more poems like Cheryl
Marie Wade's "A Night Alone":

> Longing
> tugs at my bones
> listens closely
> for his clumping braced footsteps
> on the gravel driveway
>
> ...Longing
> holds his sounds
> between my thighs
> and brings him home.[22]

More poems like Kenny Fries's "Love Poem":

> And how do you imagine me? Do you
>
> feel my callused skin? See my twisted
> bones? When you take off my clothes
>
> will you kiss me all over? Touch me as
> if my body were yours. Make me beautiful.[23]

We need more photographs like the one in JEB's collection, *Making a Way: Lesbians Out Front*. Three white women sit on a blanket
in the woods, their faces animated and smiling. Near one of the
women lies a pair of leg braces and crutches. All three women are
naked, the photo filled with a deep sense of comfort and embodiment.[24] We need more plays like *P.H.*reaks: The Hidden History of
People with Disabilities* where we see Joey, a man with cerebral palsy,
and Beth, a woman with quadriplegia, make love for the first
time.[25] We need images of heterosexual marriage, queer marriage,
one-night stands, serial monogamy, lesbian butch and femme, first
dates, enduring companionship, gay male drag, outrageous flirtation and serious commitment, all crip style. Within the context of
these images, Ellen in *Playboy* would be a non-event, Ellen on the
cover of *New Mobility* would simply be one more image, and the
ads in *Vogue* wouldn't be a site of ambivalence.

    With these images, I can begin to tunnel through my sense of
being ugly and clumsy, unattractive and undesirable. When I look
in the mirror, I can remember Joey on stage as a lover and a man

with CP, his hands grasping, speech halting, in ways that look and sound familiar. I can see myself as sexy. I can read the words of Sandra Lambert, the disabled woman in JEB's photo: "In the photos we [JEB and I] did together I am naked in an altered context—not alone, not anonymous, and beautiful."[26] Read her words and come to know the beauty in my body. With these images, I may find myself catching the eye of some attractive woman across the dance floor. But I don't want these images just for myself and other politicized crips in the movement. I want them to reach into nursing homes and rehab centers, sawmills and auto factories. I want the logger disabled in a chainsaw accident, the war vet using a wheelchair, the secretary with a repetitive stress injury so bad she can't move her hands, to be able to refigure their bodies as something other than broken, neglected, medicalized objects of pity.

~~~

But images alone are not enough. Behind the current lack of images of disabled people and our sexuality is our real, actual, institutionalized asexuality. All the same forces that relegate disabled adults to a perpetual childhood also shape us as asexual. Sheltered employment, protective paternalism, and restrictive legislation make discovering and developing the sense of an autonomous self, much less a sexual self, difficult at best. Add to this, nursing homes that forbid sexual relationships between consenting adults who live there;[27] rehabilitation centers that don't provide much of anything, much less sex education to newly disabled adults;[28] and a medical establishment that now encourages the *voluntary* sterilization of developmentally disabled adults. These institutional barriers mount up fast, combining with the attitudinal barriers, to create a profound reality of asexuality.

We are truly the genderless, asexual undesirables in the mind's eye of the nondisabled world. The forces that keep us there must change. The image of Ellen on the cover of *New Mobility*, though light years away from the images created by MDA and Mencap, is not enough. I want to add a fourth picture to my collage. Alongside the images of the empty wheelchair, the disabled adults passively posed as children, and Ellen looking sexy, let me place another black-and-white photo.

~~~

A white man looks into the camera, head tilted back just a bit, face creased with a smile. His full beard is beginning to gray, mouth slightly open as if the shutter clicked mid-sentence. A respirator tube angles out of his mouth, down his chest, high back of his wheelchair just visible behind his left shoulder. *Photograph of Ed Roberts accompanying an interview.*[29]

~~~

Ed Roberts is often called the father of the disability rights movement. Disabled by polio in 1953, Ed used a wheelchair and needed to spend a large part of each day in an iron lung. After high school and two years at San Mateo Community College, he applied to UC Berkeley. First, California's Department of Rehabilitation refused to help pay for his education. Ed's rehab counselor deemed him "unemployable, not feasible." Then UC Berkeley resisted admitting him. One dean told Ed, "We've tried cripples before, and it didn't work."[30] Finally after much struggle, both the state and the university relented, and Ed moved to UC Berkeley, living in the student infirmary at UC's Cowell Hospital because none of the dormitories had floors strong enough to support his 800-pound iron lung. Over the next several years, as Ed earned bachelors and masters degrees in political science, and soaked in the political and cultural ferment of Berkeley in the mid-'60s, a number of severely disabled men were admitted to the university and lived with him at Cowell. They dubbed themselves the Rolling Quads and started to formulate disability as a civil rights issue, setting up a network of personal attendants, and successfully insisting the city of Berkeley add curb cuts to newly built sidewalks.

By the late '60s, the Rolling Quads were tired of living at Cowell. They wanted to live in their own apartments in the community but faced huge problems trying to find wheelchair-accessible housing. Influenced by the activism of the Civil Rights movement, women's liberation, and the anti-war protests, Ed and his friends founded the Physically Disabled Students Program (PDSP) in 1970 to help disabled students live independently.

PDSP advocated for students, organized self-help groups, gathered information about accessible housing, ran a wheelchair repair shop, and helped folks find attendant services. The demand for the services of PDSP was high both on campus and off, so in 1972 the leaders of PDSP founded the Center for Independent Living (CIL) in Berkeley with Ed as its director. Since then, CILs have sprung up all over the country and have been one of the major forces in creating self-determination for disabled people. Ed went on to become the head of California's Department of Rehabilitation and a chief reformer of the institution that a mere 14 years before had declared him unemployable. The work of Ed and the Rolling Quads marked the beginning of the disability rights movement.

The focus on self-determination, on the question of who gets to control the lives of disabled people—the medical establishment or disabled people ourselves—which Ed so clearly framed and articulated in his organizing, is still central today. As I write this essay, disability activists and lobbyists are working to push federal legislation, the Medicaid Community Attendant Services Act (MiCASA), through Congress. This Act would allow disabled and old people to spend Medicaid dollars on community-based services as well as on nursing home care, essentially giving the 2.2 million people who live in nursing homes the fundamental right to choose where they want to live. As it stands now, states are required to use Medicaid funding to support nursing homes and Intermediate Care Facilities for the Mentally Retarded, but not community- and home-based services. This means that in many states disabled people can find a Medicaid-funded nursing home placement, but not Medicaid-funded (meaning affordable) attendant services, which in turn means being forced to live in an institution rather than in the community. MiCASA would begin to change all this.

Unfortunately the fundamental tenant of independent living, the right to control one's own life, is still a contested idea in the dominant culture. The movement has made headway—disabled children are more likely go to integrated schools alongside their nondisabled peers, the ADA (Americans with Disabilities Act) is providing a certain level of civil rights protection, and barrier-free access is a growing reality—but not enough. Disabled people, particularly those with severe disabilities, are still living behind locked doors, the genderless, asexual undesirables shunted away.

I look at the photo of Ed Roberts and imagine how it could have been. Rather than a portrait of Ed sitting outside his house, I conjure him in a nursing home, dressed in a nursing gown, eyes refusing the camera, Ed at the mercy of nurses and nurse's aids. I return to his picture, as it is, not as it could easily have been, and see a man happily engaged in the work of changing the world.

Does Ellen Stohl know what Ed Roberts and other disability activists have won for her? Does she know that *Playboy* wouldn't have even considered her, that *New Mobility* wouldn't even exist, without the disability rights movement? Does she understand—or for that matter do I—just how linked the struggles for self-determination and for a self-defined, recognized sexuality are? We will never find our sexualities within the confines of a nursing home or the bounds of a medical model of disability. I place Ed's engagement next to Ellen's pose. The camera catches Ed mid-sentence, Ellen arranged for an audience. I know these two images have very different intentions, but still they create a dialogue. I listen to Ed's activist passion for making independent living a reality for all disabled people. He means to overturn ableism. I watch Ellen's pose search for a place in a world that denies her sexuality, her womanhood. She means not to change Hollywood, but to break in, wheelchair and all. This tension between the one who is shaking the world up and the one who simply wants an entrance into that world shadows many marginalized, politicized communities today. Taken side by side, the images of Ed and Ellen ask questions about social change and assimilation, invisibility and representation, stereotypes and self-images, self-determination and sexuality. But in spite of the tension between them, they also merge to form the perfect retort to MDA's empty wheelchair and Mencap's vision of disabled people as passive children.

Stones in My Pockets, Stones in My Heart

Gender reaches into disability; disability wraps around class; class strains against abuse; abuse snarls into sexuality; sexuality folds on top of race ... everything finally piling into a single human body. To write about any aspect of identity, any aspect of the body, means writing about this entire maze. This I know, and yet the question remains: where to start? Maybe with my white skin, stubbly red hair, left ear pierced, shoulders set slightly off center, left riding higher than right, hands tremoring, traced with veins, legs well-muscled. Or with me in the mirror, dressing to go out, knotting my tie, slipping into my blazer, curve of hip and breast vanishing beneath my clothes. Or possibly with the memory of how my body felt swimming in the river, chinook fingerlings nibbling at my toes. There are a million ways to start, but how do I reach beneath the skin?

~~~

Age 13, hair curling down around my ears, glasses threatening to slide off my nose, I work with my father every weekend building a big wooden barn of a house. I wear overalls, my favorite flannel shirt, sleeves rolled up over a long-john top, and well-worn work boots. Over the years, my mother and I have fought about my hair. I want to cut the curls off; she thinks they're pretty. All morning I have sawed 2x12 girders to length, helped my father pound them into place. I come home from the building site to pick up a crowbar and eat lunch. A hammer hangs from my hammer loop; a utility knife rides in my bib pocket. I ask my mother, "Am I feminine?" My memory stops here. I do not remember what possessed me to ask that question, what I wanted to know, what my mother answered.

Feminine. Female. Girl. I watched my younger sister spend hours in the bathroom with a curling iron, my mother with her nail file and eyebrow tweezers. I watched and listened to the girls in my school talk about boys, go behind the equipment shed to kiss them, later whisper in algebra class about fucking them. I watched from the other side of a stone wall, a wall that was part self-preservation, part bones and blood of aloneness, part the impossible assumptions I could not shape my body around.

Dresses. Make-up. High heels. Perfume. I tried wearing the skirts my mother sewed for me. She urged me into Girl Scouts, slumber parties, the 4-H knitting and sewing clubs. I failed, not wanting any part of these activities. I loved my work boots and overalls long after all the other girls had discovered pantyhose and mini-skirts. But failing left a hole in my heart; I wanted to belong somewhere.

Am I feminine? Maybe I meant: "What am I, a girl, a boy, something else entirely?" Maybe I meant: "Can I be a girl *like this*?" Or maybe I was simply trying to say: "Mama, I don't understand." What did I want her to say? At 13, I didn't have a clue what it meant to be feminine or, for that matter, masculine. Those words were empty signifiers, important only because I knew I was suppose to have an attachment to femininity. At 13, my most sustaining relations were not in the human world. I collected stones—red, green, gray, rust, white speckled with black, black streaked with silver—and kept them in my pockets, their hard surfaces warming slowly to my body heat. Spent long days at the river learning what I could from the salmon, frogs, and salamanders. Roamed the beaches at high tide and low, starfish, mussels, barnacles clinging to the rocks. Wandered in the hills thick with moss, fern, liverwort, bramble, tree. Only here did I have a sense of body. Those stones warm in my pockets, I knew them to be the steadiest, only inviolate parts of myself. I wanted to be a hermit, to live alone with my stones and trees, neither a boy nor a girl. And now 20 years later, how do I reach beneath the skin to write, not about the stones, but the body that warmed them, the heat itself?

~~~

I could start with the ways my body has been stolen from me. Start slowly, reluctantly, with my parents. My father who raised me, his eldest daughter, as an almost son. My father who started raping me so young I can't remember when he first forced his penis into me. My mother who tells me she didn't know about his violence. I believe her because I know how her spirit vacated the premises, leaving only her body as a marker. My mother who closed her eyes and turned her back, who said to my father, "She's yours to raise as you see fit." My mother who was shaped entirely by absence and my father who taught me the hills and woods: they were the first thieves.

But tell me, if I start here by placing the issues of violence and neglect on the table alongside my queerness, what will happen next? Will my words be used against me, twisted to bolster the belief that sexual abuse causes homosexuality, contorted to provide evidence that transgressive gender identity is linked directly to neglect? Most feminist and queer activists reject these linkages and for good reason. Conservatives often use them to discredit lesbian, gay, bi, and trans identities and to argue for our conversion rather than our liberation. But this strategy of denial, rejecting any possibility of connection between abuse and gender identity, abuse and sexuality, slams a door on the messy reality of how our bodies are stolen.

~~~

I question my mother about that day when I asked, "Am I feminine?" I hope she will remember my question and her answer and offer me some clues about what I wanted to know. She has no memory of that day, but reminds me of something else. One year during the long rainy season we called winter, the Lions Club held a carnival in the old, falling-down junior high gymnasium. I wasted money on "the man-eating fish," only to see Tiny Lawrence eating tuna from a can, laughed at the boys throwing wet sponges at the volunteer firemen, then stood watching a woman draw quick cartoon-like portraits, each signed "Betsy Hammond" with a flourish. She was new to town, and I, curious, eventually paid my dollar to sit down in front of her easel. I recognized myself in the resulting drawing, liked the hard lines that defined my face, the angle of my jaw, the toughness in my mouth.

Weeks later in the grocery store, my mother introduced herself to Betsy. They started talking about husbands and children, and soon my mother mentioned me, her eldest daughter, and the portrait I had brought home from the carnival. Betsy didn't know what my mother was talking about. Finally after much confusion, she asked, "Didn't I draw your son?" I remember the complete joy I felt when my mother came home with this story. I looked again and again at the portrait, thinking, "Right here, right now, I am a boy." It made me smile secretly for weeks, reach down into my pockets to squeeze a stone tight in each fist. I felt as if I were looking in a mirror and finally seeing myself, rather than some distorted fun-house image.

~~~

How do I write not about the stones, but the heat itself? I could start by asking some hard, risky questions. Really, I'd rather hang out with my ten-year-old self and share in her moment of glee as she looked in the mirror. But truly, those questions feel inevitable, and my boyhood pleasure turns cold when I dip into the messy reality of how my body was stolen. So, whatever the risk, let me ask.

How did my father's violence, his brutal taking of me over and over again, help shape and damage my body, my sexuality, my gender identity? How did his gendered abuse—and in this culture vaginal rape is certainly gendered—reinforce my sense of not being a girl? How did his non-abusive treatment of me as an almost son interact with the ways in which his fists and penis and knives told me in no uncertain terms that I was a girl? How did watching him sexually abuse other children—both boys and girls—complicate what I knew of being girl, being boy? How did my mother's willful ignorance of the hurt he inflicted on me influence what I absorbed about femininity and masculinity?

~~~

Little did I know back then as I carried that carnival caricature home with me that the experience of being called sir, assumed to be a young man, would become a regular occurrence. This gender ambiguity, being seen as a woman at one turn and a teenage boy at the next, marks to a large extent my queerness. When people stumble over their pronouns, stammer, blush, or apologize in embarrassment, I often think of Riki Anne Wilchins' description of her friend Holly Boswell:

> Holly is a delicate Southern belle of long acquaintance.... S/he has tender features, long, wavy blonde hair, a soft Carolina accent, a delicate feminine bosom, and no interest in surgery. Holly lives as an open transgendered mother of two in Ashville, North Carolina. Her comforting advice to confused citizens struggling with whether to use Sir or Madam is, "Don't give it a second thought. You don't have a pronoun yet for me."[1]

Sometimes when I'm read as a woman, I actively miss hearing "sir," "ma'am" sounding foreign, distant, unfamiliar, even wrong to me. Usually I feel safer, somewhat buffered from men's violence against women, walking the streets after dark, knowing my nighttime outline and stride are frequently read as male. But mostly, I feel matter-of-fact: "Oh yeah, this is happening again."

Many dykes feel angered, irritated, dismayed, shamed by the experience of being read as male, feel the need to assert their womanhood. And in the same vein, I hear all the time about gay men who pump up their masculinity. To defend and strengthen one's authentic gender identity is important. But all too often I hear defensiveness in the argument that butch dykes don't mimic men but carve out new ways of being women; in the gay male personals that dismiss femmes and drag queens out of hand. Is this our one and only response to a heterosexist world that refuses to recognize feminine males and masculine females, that challenges our very queerness?

In the past decade, the burgeoning transgender/transsexual movement has questioned and started to wage a struggle against the binary gender system that automatically links female-bodied people to femininity to womanhood and male-bodied people to masculinity to manhood. Even the binary of female-bodied and male-bodied appears more and more to be a social construction as intersexed people—people who for any number of reasons are born with or develop ambiguous genitals, reproductive organs, and/or secondary sex characteristics—begin to speak publicly of their lives and the medical intrusion they've faced. How natural are the rigid, mutually exclusive definitions of male and female if they have to be defended by genital surgery performed on intersexed people? The trans movement suggests a world full of gender and sex variation, a world much more complex than one divided into female-bodied women and male-bodied men. Many trans activists argue for an end, not to the genders of woman and man, but to the socially constructed binary.

Within this context, to answer the homophobes becomes easy, those folks who want to dehumanize, erase, make invisible the lives of butch dykes and nellie fags. We shrug. We laugh. We tell them: your definitions of woman and man suck. We tell them: your binary stinks. We say: here we are in all our glory—male, female, intersexed, trans, butch, nellie, studly, femme, king, androgynous, queen, some of us carving out new ways of being women, others of us new ways of being men, and still others new ways of being something else entirely. *You don't have pronouns yet for us.*

~~~

How do I write not about the stones, but the heat itself? I could start with the brutal, intimate details of my father's thievery, of his hands clamping around my neck, tearing into me, claiming my body as his own. The brutal, intimate details, but listen: I get afraid that the homophobes are right, that maybe in truth I live as a transgendered butch because he raped me, my mother neglected me. I lose the bigger picture, forget that woven through and around the private and intimate is always the public and political.

We live in a time of epidemic child abuse, in a world where sexual and physical violence against children isn't only a personal tragedy and a symptom of power run amok, but also a form of social control. When a father rapes his daughter, a mother beats her son, a white schoolteacher sexually fondles a Black student, a middle-class man uses a working-class boy to make child pornography, a nondisabled caregiver leaves a disabled kid to sit in her/his urine for hours, these adults teach children bodily lessons about power and hierarchy, about being boys, being girls, being children, being Black, being working-class, being disabled.

What better way to maintain a power structure—white supremacy, male supremacy, capitalism, a binary and rigid gender system—than to drill the lessons of who is dominant and who is subordinate into the bodies of children. No, not every individual perpetrator thinks, "This kid has stepped too far outside. I need to beat/rape her back into line." But certainly the power imbalances out of which child abuse arises are larger than any individual perpetrator's conscious intentions. Social control happens exactly at the junctures where the existing power structure is—consciously or not—maintained and strengthened.

And here is the answer to my fear. Child abuse is not the cause of but rather a response to—among other things—transgressive gender identity and/or sexuality. The theory I'm trying to shape is not as simple as "My father abused me because I was a queer child who—by the time I had any awareness of gender—was not at all sure of my girlness," although some genderqueer kids do get raped specifically because of their queerness. Rather I want to say, "My father raped me for many reasons, and inside his acts of violence I learned about what it meant to be female, to be a child, to live in my particular body, and those lessons served the larger power structure and hierarchy well."

~~~

At the same time, our bodies are not merely blank slates upon which the powers-that-be write their lessons. We cannot ignore the body itself: the sensory, mostly non-verbal experience of our hearts and lungs, muscles and tendons, telling us and the world who we are. My childhood sense of being neither girl nor boy arose in part from the external lessons of abuse and neglect, from the confusing messages about masculinity and femininity that I could not comprehend; I would be a fool to claim otherwise. But just as certainly, there was a knowing that resided in my bones, in the stretch of my legs and arch of my back, in the stones lying against my skin, a knowing that whispered, "not girl, not boy."

Butch, nellie, studly, femme, king, androgynous, queen: how
have we negotiated the lies and thievery, the ways gender is influenced by divisions of labor, by images of masculinity and femininity, by racism, sexism, classism, ableism, by the notions of "real"
men and "real" women? And how, at the same time, have we listened to our own bodies? For me the answer is not simple.

I think about my disabled body. For too long, I hated my
trembling hands, my precarious balance, my spastic muscles so repeatedly overtaken by tension and tremor, tried to hide them at all
costs. More than once I wished to amputate my right arm so it
wouldn't shake. Self-mutilation is shame of the baldest kind. All
the lies contained in the words *retard, monkey, defect*; in the gawking,
the pats on my head, and the tears cried on my shoulder; in the
moments where I became someone's supercrip or tragedy: all those
lies became my second skin.

I think about my disabled body, how as a teenager I escaped
the endless pressure to have a boyfriend, to shave my legs, to wear
make-up. The same lies that cast me as genderless, asexual, and
undesirable also framed a space in which I was left alone to be my
quiet, bookish, tomboy self, neither girl nor boy. Even then, I was
grateful. But listen, if I had wanted to date boys, wear lipstick and
mascara, play with feminine clothes—the silk skirt and pumps, the
low-cut blouse, the outrageous prom dress—I would have had to
struggle much longer and harder than my nondisabled counterparts. The sheer physical acts of shaving my legs and putting on
make-up would have been hard enough. Harder still would have
been the relentless arguing with my parents, resisting their image
of me as asexual or vulnerable to assault, persuading them that I
could in truth take care of myself at the movies with Brent Miller
or Dave Wilson.[2] But in truth I didn't want to date Brent or wear
the low-cut blouse. I shuddered at the thought. How would I have
reacted to the gendered pressures my younger, nondisabled sister
faced? For her the path of least resistance pointed in the direction
of femininity; for me it led toward not-girl-not-boy. But to cast my
abiding sense of gendered self simply as a reaction to ableism is to
ignore my body and what it had to tell me. When I look around
me in disability community, I see an amazing range of gender expression, running the gamut from feminine to androgynous to

masculine, mixed and swirled in many patterns. Clearly we respond in a myriad of ways to the ableist construction of gender.

How do we negotiate the lies and listen to our bodies? I think about my disabled body, my queer butch body read as a teenage boy. The markers of masculinity—my shaved head and broad stance, direct gaze and muscled arms—are unmistakable. And so are the markers of disability—my heavy-heeled gait; my halting, uneven speech; the tremors in my hands, arms, and shoulders. They all twine together to shape me in the ableist world as either genderless or a teenage boy. The first is all too familiar to disabled people. The second arises from the gender binary, where if I am not recognized as a woman, then I am presumed to be a man or more likely, given my lack of height and facial hair, a teenage boy. These external perceptions match in large part my internal sense of gender, my bodily comfort with gender ambiguity. But if the external and internal didn't match, what then?

Once I sat in a writing workshop with straight, feminine, disabled women, and we talked for an entire afternoon about gender identity, precisely because of the damage inflicted when the external ableist perceptions don't match the internal sense of self. All too often, the thieves plant their lies, and our bodies absorb them as the only truth. Is it any surprise that sometimes my heart fills with small gray stones, which never warm to my body heat?

~~~

The work of thieves: certainly external perception, stereotypes, lies, false images, and oppression hold a tremendous amount of power. They define and create who we are, how we think of our bodies, our gendered selves. How do I write not about the stones, but the body that warms them, the heat itself? That question haunts me because I lived by splitting body from mind, body from consciousness, body from physical sensation, body from emotion as the bullies threw rocks and called *retard,* as my father and his buddies tied me down, pulled out their knives. My body became an empty house, one to which I seldom returned. I lived in exile; the stones rattling in my heart, resting in my pockets, were my one and only true body.

But just as the stolen body exists, so does the reclaimed body. I think of disabled people challenging the conception of a "perfect" body/mind. Ed Roberts sits out front of his house talking about crip liberation. Ellen Stohl shapes herself into a sex symbol for the disability community. I think of queer people pushing upon the dominant culture's containment of gender, pleasure, and sex. Drag queens and kings work the stage. Dykes take to the streets. Gay men defend public sex. Trans people of all varieties say, "This is how we can be men, women, how we can inhabit all the spaces in between." Radical faeries swirl in their pagan finery. Bisexual people resist a neat compartmentalizing of sexuality. I think of people of color, poor people, working-class people all thumbing their noses at the notion of assimilation. Over and over again, we take the lies and crumble them into dust.

But how do I write about *my* body reclaimed, full of pride and pleasure? It is easy to say that abuse and ableism and homophobia stole my body away, broke my desire, removed me from my pleasure in the stones warm against my skin, the damp sponginess of moss growing on a rotten log, the taste of spring water dripping out of rock. Harder to express how that break becomes healed, a bone once fractured, now whole, but different from the bone never broken. And harder still to follow the path between the two. How do I mark this place where my body is no longer an empty house, desire whistling lonely through the cracks, but not yet a house fully lived in? For me the path from stolen body to reclaimed body started with my coming out as a dyke.

~~~

I was 18 and had just moved to the city. I didn't want to be a girl, nor was I a boy. I hid my body, tried as much as possible to ignore it. During my first week of college, I started meeting dykes. In three weeks I began asking, "Am I a lesbian?" Once before, I had faced this question and known the answer. The summer I was 12, two women, friends of my parents, came visiting from Arkansas. I adored Suzanne and Susan, showed them my favorite spots, the best blackberry brambles, where the muskrat built her den. I wanted them to stay with me in my river valley. They came out to my parents, and later I overheard my father say that Suzanne was gay, his face growing tight and silent. Somehow I knew what that word meant, even though I barely understood *homosexual* and had only heard *lesbian* as a taunt. It made me smile. The image of Suzanne and Susan holding hands as we walked Battle Rock Beach stuck with me for weeks. I knew somewhere deep inside me, rising up to press against my sternum, that I was like them. This I knew, but by the time I turned 13, it had vanished.

Now at the age of 18, I picked the question up again. I had never kissed a boy, never had a boyfriend or girlfriend. I knew nothing about sexual desire. For me sex was bound together with abuse. I had learned the details from my father just as I had learned how to mix a wheelbarrow of concrete, frame a stud wall. Sex meant rape—that simple, that complicated. The only thing I knew about desire was the raw, split-openness that rampaged through me after he was done, how those feelings could overtake my body again late at night in my own bed, mounting up uncontainably. I was not in love with a woman; I didn't even have a crush. And yet the question "Am I a lesbian?" hung with me.

I went to dyke events, read dyke books, listened to dyke music, hung out at my first dyke bar, went to my first dyke dance. I adored watching those women talk, laugh, hold hands, dance, kiss. Those soft butch women who would never have claimed their butchness then, during the lesbian-feminist androgyny of the '70s and early '80s. Those women with buzzed hair and well-defined biceps, jeans faded and soft. Those women who looked me in the eye. Watching them was like polishing my favorite stone to its brightest glint. I knew I could be *this* kind of woman and so slowly over the course of that year came to know myself as a dyke. I waited another four years to kiss a woman.

My coming out wasn't as much about discovering sexual desire and knowledge as it was about dealing with gender identity. Simply put, the disabled, mixed-class tomboy who asked her mother, "Am I feminine?" didn't discover a sexuality among dykes, but rather a definition of woman large enough to be comfortable for many years. And if that definition hadn't been large enough, what then? Would I have sought out hormones and/or surgery? If I had been born a hundred years ago when a specifically lesbian definition didn't exist, would I have been a "passing woman"? If I live long enough to see the world break free of the gender binary, will I find home not as a butch dyke, a woman by default, but as some third, fourth, fifth gender? Some gender that seems more possible since trans people have started to organize, build community, speak out about our lives. Some gender that I have already started reaching toward.

~~~

In queer community, I found a place to belong and abandoned my desire to be a hermit. Among crips, I learned how to embrace my strong, spastic body. Through feminist work around sexual violence—political activism, theoretical analysis, emotional recovery—I came to terms with the sexual abuse and physical torture done to me. And somewhere along the line, I pulled desire to the surface, gave it room to breathe. Let me write not about the stones, but the heat itself.

I think of the first woman I dated. She and I spent many nights eating pizza, watching movies, and talking halfway until dawn. I fell in love but never even kissed her, too afraid to even say, "This is what I want," much less to lean over and put my lips to hers. It made sense only years later when my memories of rape came flooding back. I think of the butch woman, once my lover, now a good friend. One night as we lay in bed, she told me, "I like when your hands tremble over my body. It feels good, like extra touching." Her words pushed against the lies. But all too often, sex was a bodiless, mechanical act for me as I repeatedly fled my body. We decided we'd be happier as friends. I think of the woman who called me her dream butchy *shiksa* and made me smile. I took so long to realize what had flared between us she almost gave up waiting. With her, desire traced my body, vivid and unmistakable, returning me to the taste of spring water, the texture of tree bark as I climbed toward sky. With her, I understood finally what it meant to want my hand on a lover's skin, the weight of a lover's body against mine. A bone long fractured, now mending.

I turn my pockets and heart inside out, set the stones—quartz, obsidian, shale, agate, scoria, granite—along the scoured top of the wall I once lived behind, the wall I still use for refuge. They shine in the sun, some translucent to the light, others dense, solid, opaque. I lean my body into the big unbreakable expanse, tracing which stones need to melt, which will crack wide, geode to crystal, and which are content just as they are.

~~~

But before I make it too simple, let me tell another story about coming to queer community, queer identity. Five or six years after I came out, I lived in Oakland, California, still learning the habits and manners of urban dykes. I remember a weekend when 20 of us, mostly dykes, helped move a friend from north Oakland to west Berkeley. The apartment filled with laughter as we carried endless boxes to the moving van, flexed our muscles over the couch, teased the lovers who sneaked a kiss in the empty closet. That mix of friends, lovers, and ex-lovers, butch dykes, femme dykes, androgynous dykes: we elbowed and jostled and gossiped. Leslie and I hauled a table to the van. On our way back, she off-handedly said how she was glad to be wearing her steel-toed boots, but that her feet were beginning to hurt. I wanted to get to know Leslie better. She was butch and knew it. I liked watching her from across the room, feeling something less than attraction but more than curiosity. I hadn't yet named myself butch but knew I had much in common with Leslie's butchness. So when she mentioned her steel-toed boots, I asked where she worked, assuming she'd have a story about forklifts or hi-los, a warehouse, bailer, mill, factory, or mine. I thought about the summer I was 15 working in the woods. I was the only girl who started the summer with work boots already broken in. The other girls envied me for weeks as they nursed their blistered feet. Leslie said, "I just bought them as a fashion statement." I felt as if I'd been exposed as a hick yet again, caught assuming she was someone I might have grown up with. *A fashion statement.* What did I have in common with Leslie? I felt the stones in my heart grind deep.

Today, more than decade after watching Leslie from across the room, I have settled into a certain butch identity. Often I don't feel drawn to the urban markers of being butch—the leather jacket, the steel-toed boots, the black-on-black look, the arc of chain from wallet to belt loop—but I do understand how certain clothes make me feel inside my body. I learned to dress by watching the loggers and fishermen I grew up around, learned to love t-shirts and torn jeans, dusty work boots and faded flannel shirts from them. The girls with whom I went to school also wore their share of flannel and denim, but when it came time to learn how to dress like "women," they turned to *Vogue* and *Glamour*. To emulate the dress of their working-class mothers was somehow shameful. They wanted their lessons to come from the middle- and upper-class beauty mags. The boys on the other hand never thought to dress like anyone except the working-class men around them. For me, *Vogue* and *Glamour* held none of the appeal that Walt Maya did, dressed in his checked shirt, cowboy boots, and wide-brimmed hat. I joined the boys in their emulation.

I knew early on the feel of boots and denim, knew I would never learn to walk in a skirt. I loved how my body felt as I swung an ax, how my mind felt as I worked through the last and hardest algebra problem in Mr. Johnson's advanced math class, the most elusive metaphor in Mr. Beckman's poetry class. I knew I never wanted a child or a husband. I knew these things but could never have put words to them, knew them in spite of all that stole me away from my body.

How did I "know" I never wanted a husband, would never learn to walk in a skirt? What does it mean when I write that I "felt" like neither a girl nor a boy? The words *know* and *feel* are slippery in their vagueness. I pull out an old photo of myself from the night of my high school graduation. I stand outside on our front deck; behind me are the deep greens of western Oregon in May. I wear a white dress, flowers embroidered on the front panel, the plainest, simplest dress my mother would let me buy. I look painfully uncomfortable, as if I have no idea what to do with my body, hands clasped awkwardly behind me, shoulders caved inward, immobilized, almost fearful beneath my smile. I am in clumsy, unconsenting drag. This is one of the last times I wore a dress. This is my body's definition of *know* and *feel*.

And yet those things I knew and felt were also deeply shaped and colored by the rural, white, working-class culture of Port Orford. They were cradled not so much by an unconscious baby butch sensibility, but in a working-class town where at weddings and funerals everyone looked as if they had been stuffed into their dress clothes. They were nurtured in the small town hardware store and lumber yard, where, even though George always asked if I could handle the 50-pound bags of cement, I was Bob's eccentric, "handicapped" kid and was never told to stop. They were underlined by my parents' desperate upward scramble toward the middle class and their corresponding passion for formal education. They were molded by the common knowledge that most of the girls in town would catch their lives on too many kids, most of the boys on alcohol and guns, and only a few of us would leave the county for good.

~~~

The stolen body, the reclaimed body, the body that knows itself and the world, the stone and the heat which warms it: my body has never been singular. Disability snarls into gender. Class wraps around race. Sexuality strains against abuse. *This* is how to reach beneath the skin.

Friday nights I go to the local queer bar, nurse a single Corona, hang out with my dyke friends. Mostly I go to watch one of the wait staff, a woman with long brown hair, sharp nose, and ready smile. She flirts with everyone, moving table to table, making eye contact, hunkering down to have a quiet word or laugh amidst the noise. She flirts with me too, catching me in her wide smile, appreciative gaze. I am under no illusion: this is simply how she works her job. But after a lifetime of numbness I adore her attention, adore tipping back my chair, spreading my legs wide, and watching her from across the room.

I want to take the stone between my tremoring hands—trembling with CP, with desire, with the last remnants of fear, trembling because this is how my body moves—and warm it gentle, but not, as I have always done before, ride roughshod over it. I want to enter as a not-girl-not-boy transgendered butch—gendered differently than when I first came out, thinking simply, "*This* is how I'll be a woman," never imagining there might be a day when the word *woman* was too small; differently from the tomboy who wanted to be a hermit; but still connected to both. Enter with my pockets and heart half-full of stone. Enter knowing that the muscled grip of desire is a wild, half-grown horse, ready to bolt but too curious to stay away.

~~~

In the end, I will sit on the wide, flat top of my wall, legs dangling over those big, uncrackable stones, weathered smooth and clean. Sit with butch women, femme dykes, nellie men, studly fags, radical faeries, drag queens and kings, transsexual people who want nothing more than to be women and men, intersexed people, hermaphrodites with attitudes, transgendered, pangendered, bigendered, polygendered, ungendered, androgynous people of many varieties and trade stories long into the night. Laugh and cry and tell stories. Sad stories about bodies stolen, bodies no longer here. Enraging stories about false images, devastating lies, untold violence. Bold, brash stories about reclaiming our bodies and changing the world.

Notes

The Mountain

1 Quoted in Hevey, David, *The Creatures Time Forgot: Photography and Disability Imagery* (London: Routledge, 1992), p. 9.

2 Quoted in Hevey, p. 9.

3 Russell, Marta, *Beyond Ramps* (Monroe, Maine: Common Courage Press, 1998), p. 96-108.

4 Sobsey, Dick, *Violence and Abuse in the Lives of People with Disabilities* (Baltimore: Paul H. Brookes Publishing, 1994), p. 68.

5 Shapiro, Joseph, *No Pity: People with Disabilities Forging a New Civil Rights Movement* (New York: Times Books, 1994), p. 27-28.

Clearcut: Explaining the Distance

1 Devall, Bill, ed., *Clearcut: The Tragedy of Industrial Forestry* (San Francisco: Sierra Club Books and Earth Island Press, 1994).

2 Devall, Bill, ed., p. 106.

3 Logger's slang for bulldozer.

4 Foreman, Dave, *Ecodefense: A Field Guide to Monkeywrenching* (Tucson: Ned Ludd Books, 1985).

Losing Home

1 Elliott, "Whenever I Tell You the Language We Use is a Class Issue, You Nod Your Head in Agreement – And Then You Open Your Mouth" in *Out of the Class Closet: Lesbians Speak*, Penelope, Julia, ed. (Freedom, California: The Crossing Press, 1994), p. 277.

2 Elliott, p. 278.

3 Elliott, p. 280.

4 Pharr, Suzanne, "Rural Organizing: Building Community Across Difference," *Sojourner: The Women's Forum*, 19.10, 1994, p. 14.

Clearcut: Brutes and Bumper Stickers

1 Forest Action Network, "Violent Attack on Activists in British Columbia," *Earth First! Journal*, 14.5, 1994, p. 28.

Clearcut: End of the Line

1 Legally logs cut from private and state lands can be exported, but logs cut from federal lands cannot be.

Casino: An Epilogue

1   For more information on social ecology, deep ecology, and the tension between them, see Chase, Steve, ed. *Defending the Earth: A Dialogue Between Murray Bookchin and Dave Foreman* (Boston: South End Press, 1991). For an excellent analysis of class, union organizing, and radical environmental activism, see Bari, Judi, *Timber Wars* (Monroe, Maine: Common Courage Press, 1994).

2   Durbin, Kathie, *Tree Huggers: Victory, Defeat, and Renewal in the Northwest Ancient Forest Campaign* (Seattle: The Mountaineers, 1996), p. 184.

Queers and Freaks

1   The word *handicap* means to compensate each participant in a contest differently in order to equalize the chances of winning and derives from a lottery game called "hand in cap," in which players held forfeits in a cap. In spite of this derivation, the word play "cap in hand" resonates ironically with the ways in which disabled people have survived as beggars.

2   Mairs, Nancy, *Plaintext* (Tucson: University of Arizona Press, 1986), p. 9.

3   Mairs, p. 10.

4   *Freak* actually is used by a number of marginalized peoples: hippies, drug users, and l/g/b/t people, as well as disabled people.

5   *Pervert* is sometimes used by queer people in leather and s/m communities who feel marginalized within the larger queer culture. The point here isn't that *pervert* and *retard* are never spoken with affection or pride but that they haven't been embraced and used to construct both individual and communal identities.

6   Thomson, Rosemarie Garland, *Extraordinary Bodies: Figuring Physical Disability in American Culture and Literature* (New York: Columbia University Press, 1997), p. 62-63.

7   Bogdan, Robert, *Freak Show: Presenting Human Oddities for Amusement and Profit* (Chicago: University of Chicago Press, 1988), p. 136.

8   Quoted in Merish, Lori, "Cuteness and Commodity Aesthetics: Tom Thumb and Shirley Temple" in *Freakery: Cultural Spectacles of the Extraordinary Body,* Thomson, Rosemarie Garland, ed. (New York: New York University Press, 1996), p. 190.

9   Bogdan, p. 268.

10   Quoted in Shapiro, p. 59.

11   Kadi, Joanna, *Thinking Class: Sketches from a Cultural Worker* (Boston: South End Press, 1996), p. 103.

12   For instance, before the end of slavery, slave children born disabled were often sold to showmen, sometimes for large sums of money. Conjoined twins Millie and Christina (last name unknown), born into slavery in 1852, brought their master $30,000.

13   Quoted in Lindfors, Beruth, "Circus Africans," *Journal of American Culture,* 6.2, 1983, p. 9.

14 Vogt, Carl in *Freakery,* p. 158.

15 Oliver, Michael, *The Politics of Disablement* (New York: St. Martin's Press, 1990), p. 48.

16 Bogdan, p. 230.

17 Vaughan, Christopher, "Ogling Igorots" in *Freakery,* p. 222.

18 This year-long celebration, marking the 500th year anniversary of Christopher Columbus's arrival in the Americas, focused on people of color's ongoing resistance to racism, imperialism, and genocide.

19 *The Couple in the Cage: A Guatinaui Odyssey* (video) (Authentic Documentary Productions, 1993).

20 Quoted in Bogdan, p.173.

21 Shapiro, p. 63-64.

22 Bogdan, p. 280.

23 Blumberg, Lisa, "Public Stripping" in *The Ragged Edge: The Disability Experience from the Pages of the First Fifteen Years of The Disability Rag,* Shaw, Barrett, ed. (Louisville, Kentucky: Avocado Press, 1994), p. 73-77.

24 Blumberg, Lisa, "Public Stripping Revisited," *The Disability Rag,* 17.3, 1996, p. 18-21.

25 Baizley, Doris, and Lewis, Victoria Ann, adapted from a writing workshop, *Ph*reaks: The Hidden History of People with Disabilities* (Unpublished manuscript, c/o Helen Merrill, 235 West 23 St. (1A), New York, NY 10011), p. 9.

26 "Nearly Half of Us Don't Know About the ADA, Says New Harris Poll," *Ragged Edge,* 19.5, 1998, p. 5.

27 Shapiro, p. 28.

28 ADAPT (American Disabled for Attendant Programs Today) can be reached at 1339 Lamar Sq. Dr., #101, Austin, TX 78204. Phone: 512-442-0252. E-mail address: adapt@adapt.org.

29 Not Dead Yet can be reached at Progress CIL, 7521 Madison St., Forest Park, IL 60130. Contact: Diane Coleman. Phone: 708-209-1500. TTY: 708-209-1826.

30 Shapiro, p. 66-70.

31 Jewish gay men were likely to be marked as Jews first.

Reading Across the Grain

1 "We Wish We Wouldn't See...," *The Disability Rag,* 13.5, 1992, p. 46.

2 Maddox, Sam, "The Seven Year Itch," *New Mobility,* 5.15, 1994. Christopher Voelker, photographer.

3 Hevey, plate 5.

4 "Meet Ellen Stohl," *Playboy,* 34.7,1987, p. 67-74.

5 "Meet Ellen Stohl," p. 68.

6 Longmore, Paul, "The Second Phase: From Disability Rights to Disability Culture," *The Disability Rag,* 16.5, 1995, p. 8-9.

7 Shapiro, p. 143, 208.

8 Shapiro, p. 289-321.

9   Sobsey, p. 119-20.

10   Waxman, Barbara Faye, "It's Time to Politicize Our Sexual Oppression" in *The Ragged Edge*, p. 83.

11   Shapiro, p. 255-56.

12   Shapiro, p. 238.

13   Kiss and Tell, *Her Tongue on My Theory* (Vancouver, B.C.: Press Gang Publishers, 1994), p. 80.

14   Panzarino, Connie, *The Me in the Mirror* (Seattle: Seal Press, 1994), p. 212.

15   Shapiro, p. 39.

16   Shapiro, p. 40.

17   Poor women hear this argument, that they are being irresponsible by being pregnant, all the time. In the case of poor, nondisabled women the argument leads to the presumption that they are loose and promiscuous by nature. For disabled women the argument leads in a slightly different direction, that the immorality of potentially reproducing their disabilities proves they shouldn't be sexual.

18   Finger, Anne, "In Vogue," *The Disability Rag*, 16.4, 1996, p. 33

19   Finger, p. 33.

20   Kiss and Tell, p. 51.

21   Finger, Anne, "Helen and Frida" in *Staring Back: The Disability Experience from the Inside Out*, Fries, Kenny, ed. (New York: Plume, 1997), p. 255-63.

22   Wade, Cheryl Marie, "A Night Alone," *The Disability Rag*, 13.5, 1992, p. 36.

23   Fries, Kenny, *Anesthesia* (Louisville, Kentucky: Avocado Press, 1996), p. 10.

24   Biren, Joan E., *Making a Way: Lesbians Out Front* (Washington, D.C.: Glad Hag Books, 1987), plate 20.

25   Baizley and Lewis, p. 45-48.

26   Biren, plate 20.

27   Waxman, p. 84.

28   Gwin, Lucy, "Auschwitz on Sesame Street" in *The Ragged Edge*, p. 178-85.

29   Gwin, Lucy, "Ed Roberts: We're Talking About Inclusion Here," *New Mobility*, 5.15, 1994, p. 43. Lydia Gans, photographer.

30   Shapiro, p. 45.

Stones in My Pockets, Stones in My Heart

1   Wilchins, Riki Anne, *Read My Lips* (Ithaca, New York: Firebrand Books, 1997), p. 118.

2   I now recognize the disturbing irony of this, given the ways in which my father was sexually using me.

Index

About the Author

Eli Clare is a poet, essayist, and activist living in Ann Arbor, Michigan. Her writing has been published widely, under her given name Elizabeth Clare, in periodicals including *Sinister Wisdom, Evergreen Chronicles, Sojourner: The Women's Forum, The Disability Rag,* and *Hanging Loose,* and anthologies such as *My Lover Is a Woman: Contemporary Lesbian Love Poems* (Ballentine Books), *Queerly Classed: Gay Men and Lesbians Write about Class* (South End Press), *Staring Back: The Disability Experience from the Inside Out* (Plume), and *Cultural Activisms: Poetic Voices, Political Voices* (SUNY).

About South End Press

South End Press is a nonprofit, collectively run book publisher with over 200 titles in print. Since our founding in 1977, we have tried to meet the needs of readers who are exploring, or are already committed to, the politics of radical social change. Our goal is to publish books that encourage critical thinking and constructive action on the key political, cultural, social, economic, and ecological issues shaping life in the United States and in the world. In this way, we hope to give expression to a wide diversity of democratic social movements and to provide an alternative to the products of corporate publishing.

Through the Institute for Social and Cultural Change, South End Press works with other political media projects—*Z Magazine*; Speakout, a speakers' bureau; and Alternative Radio—to expand access to information and critical analysis. For a free catalog of South End Press books, please write to us at: South End Press, 7 Brookline St., Cambridge MA 02139. Visit our website at http://www.lbbs.org/sep/sep.htm.

Related Titles from South End Press

Queerly Classed: Gay Men and Lesbians Write about Class
Edited by Susan Raffo
$17.00 paper; $40.00 cloth

Thinking Class: Sketches from a Cultural Worker
by Joanna Kadi
$14.00 paper; $40.00 cloth

The Last Generation: Poetry and Prose
by Cherríe Moraga
$14.00 paper; $30.00 cloth

Memoir of a Race Traitor
by Mab Segrest
$15.00 paper; $30.00 cloth

The Queer Question: Essays on Desire and Democracy
by Scott Tucker
$18.00 paper; $40.00 cloth

Policing Public Sex: Queer Politics and the Future of AIDS Activism
Edited by Dangerous Bedfellows
$20.00 paper; $40.00 cloth

Culture Clash: The Making of Gay Sensibility
by Michael Bronski
$17.00 paper; $30.00 cloth

Walking to The Edge: Essays of Resistance
by Margaret Randall
$12.00 paper; $25.00 cloth

Women, AIDS and Activism
by the ACT UP/NY Women and AIDS Book Group
$9.00 paper; $25.00 cloth
Also available in Spanish as *La Mujer, el SIDA y el Activismo*
$10.00 paper; $30.00 cloth

When ordering, please include $3.50 for postage and handling for the first book
and 50 cents for each additional book.
To order by credit card, call 1-800-533-8478.